Girls Need Good Credit Too

Monthly Planner for Establishing and
Maintaining Good Credit

DR. DONNA PRUDHOMME

Written by Dr. Donna Prudhomme
Illustrated by Charlotte Pabalan

Printed in the United States of America
ISBN 978-1-7331188-9-7

www.crediteducationschool.com
info@crediteducationschool.com

Disclaimer

The author is not a lawyer. For legal advice, please seek an attorney as the contents of this book should not be construed as legal advice in any way. Every effort has been made to ensure the accuracy of the information within this book. However, we cannot be held liable for any omissions, errors, or inconsistencies. You are solely responsible for actions taken (or not taken) based on the information contained in this book.

This planner belongs to

____

Contents

Dedication

This planner is dedicated to my beloved sister, Nasheka Powell, affectionately known as Shay. Your presence is deeply missed every day, but I feel your spirit guiding me on this journey.

I ♡ Love you Sissy

Acknowledgements

First and foremost, I want to thank God for the opportunity to educate and empower girls around the world about the importance of credit.

I am deeply grateful to my loving husband, whose unwavering support has been a cornerstone of all my endeavors. You witnessed my exhaustion and the challenges of failed business ventures, yet you never told me to give up. I remember you saying, "You are always working hard, and eventually, something will happen." Your belief in me has been a constant source of strength and encouragement.

To my son and daughter, every pursuit I've undertaken has been for you, with the hope of making your lives better. Thank you for your patience and encouragement, especially during the times when things didn't go as planned. You have witnessed my struggles, and I am confident that you have learned from my mistakes. Your strength and resilience continue to inspire me, and I know these experiences will make you both even stronger.

Hey Girl, Hey!

This planner was created with you in mind. It's your monthly guide to understanding the importance of good credit, learning how to build it, and maintaining it for a brighter financial future.

Learning about credit early on is crucial, but unfortunately, many schools don't provide adequate education on this essential topic. Understanding how to build and manage credit, and how it impacts your life, is a key part of financial literacy that can shape your future opportunities and stability.

After my son and daughter graduated from high school, they were flooded with credit card offers. Reflecting on my own experience, I realized how little we discussed credit when I was growing up. My parents didn't talk to me about credit until credit card statements started arriving while I was in college. I'm incredibly thankful they intervened before I could make any major mistakes.

When I was in college, companies were all over campus, pushing credit cards on us without warning us about the potential downsides. As a naive college student, I didn't fully grasp the long-term impact on my credit score and financial health. It wasn't until later that I understood the true cost of those seemingly innocent decisions. This experience has motivated me to educate others so they can make informed choices and avoid the same pitfalls.

With over 27 years of experience as an educator, I'm dedicated to preparing not just my children but also other girls, young women, and women for the financial realities of life. This planner is a tool to help you establish and maintain good credit, navigate the financial landscape confidently, and make informed decisions that will benefit you for years to come.

Empower yourself with knowledge and take control of your financial future. Remember, good credit isn't just about numbers–it's about freedom, opportunities, and peace of mind.

Dr. Donna Prudhomme

Dr. Donna Prudhomme
Board Certified Credit Consultant

“Credit is like a superpower—use it wisely, and you can achieve anything!”

Introduction

As you step into adulthood, there's one topic that will play a huge role in shaping your future: credit. Whether you realize it or not, credit impacts many aspects of life—buying a car, renting an apartment, even landing a job. But here's the surprising thing: most of us aren't taught about credit in school, even though it's one of the most important tools we need to navigate life's big decisions.

So, why is credit so important? Credit is all about trust. It's a way for people, businesses, and financial institutions to know if they can trust you with money. Good credit shows that you're responsible and reliable with your finances, while poor credit can make things like buying a car or renting your first apartment much more difficult.

Unfortunately, credit isn't something we learn about in math class or even during life skills courses. For many people, the first time they hear about credit is when they've already made mistakes that are hard to undo. So, why don't schools teach credit? The answer isn't simple, but part of the problem is that personal finance hasn't always been a priority in traditional education. Schools focus on subjects like English, math, science, and history—important topics, of course—but often leave out financial education, even though it's something everyone will need in the real world.

The lack of credit education in school means many people don't understand how credit works until it's too late. Learning about credit early—while you're still in high school—can make all the difference. Starting with the basics now will help you avoid common mistakes and prepare you to build a solid financial future.

Understanding credit gives you power. It empowers you to make smart financial decisions, plan for the future, and avoid the stress that comes from not knowing how to manage money. By taking the time to learn about credit now, you're giving yourself a head start on the rest of your life. You'll be ahead of the curve, ready to handle whatever comes your way, and prepared to build the financial freedom you deserve.

Let's dive in and explore the world of credit together. The sooner you understand how credit works, the more control you'll have over your future!

PART ONE

Understanding Credit

What is Credit?

Credit is an agreement in which a borrower receives something of value now and agrees to repay the lender at a later date, typically with interest. It is a way to access funds or goods in advance, with the promise of paying back the debt over time. Credit is crucial for making significant purchases, such as a car or home, and it plays a significant role in various aspects of financial life.

Key Elements of Credit

- **Borrowing:** When you use credit, you're essentially borrowing money or receiving goods/services with the agreement to pay back the value in the future. This can happen through various forms such as credit cards, personal loans, or mortgages.

- **Interest:** Most credit arrangements involve interest, which is the cost of borrowing money. It's typically expressed as a percentage of the amount borrowed and is added to the repayment amount.

- **Credit Score:** Your credit score is a numerical representation of your creditworthiness. It's calculated based on your credit history and indicates how likely you are to repay borrowed money. A higher score can help you get better terms on loans and credit cards.

- **Credit Report:** This is a detailed record of your credit history, including the types of credit you've used, the amounts owed, your payment history, and more. Lenders use this report to assess your risk as a borrower.

Types of Credit

- **Revolving Credit:** This type includes credit cards and lines of credit. You have a maximum limit, and you can borrow up to that limit. As you repay, the available credit renews, hence the term "revolving."

- **Installment Credit:** This type involves borrowing a fixed amount of money and repaying it with interest in regular installments over a set period. Examples include student loans, car loans, and mortgages.

Why Credit is Important

- **Financial Flexibility:** Credit allows you to make significant purchases and pay for them over time, which can be essential for large expenses like education, housing, or emergency needs.

- **Building a Credit History:** Using credit responsibly helps you build a positive credit history, which is crucial for obtaining favorable loan terms in the future. It demonstrates your ability to manage debt and repay it on time.

- **Access to Better Financial Products:** A good credit score can qualify you for lower interest rates, higher credit limits, and better terms on loans and credit cards, saving you money in the long run.

- **Renting and Employment:** Landlords and some employers check credit reports to assess reliability and financial responsibility. A strong credit history can help you secure housing and job opportunities.

Managing Credit Responsibly

- **Pay on Time:** Ensure that you make all payments by the due date to avoid penalties and negative impacts on your credit score.

- **Keep Balances Low:** Use a small portion of your available credit to maintain a healthy credit utilization ratio.

- **Limit New Credit Applications:** Each application can result in a hard inquiry on your credit report, which may lower your score temporarily.

- **Monitor Your Credit Report:** Regularly review your credit report for accuracy and dispute any errors you find.

Understanding and managing credit wisely is essential for financial health and achieving long-term financial goals.

What is FICO?

FICO, which stands for **Fair Isaac Corporation**, is a data analytics company that is best known for creating the FICO credit score. This score is a widely used measure of creditworthiness, helping lenders assess the risk of lending money to individuals.

What is a Credit Score?

A credit score is a numerical representation of your creditworthiness, which lenders use to evaluate the risk of lending you money. It reflects your credit history and provides a snapshot of your financial responsibility. The most commonly used credit scores are calculated by FICO (Fair Isaac Corporation) and VantageScore.

How is a Credit Score Calculated?

Credit scores are calculated based on the information in your credit report. The exact formulas are proprietary, but the main factors considered and their typical weightings for a FICO score are:

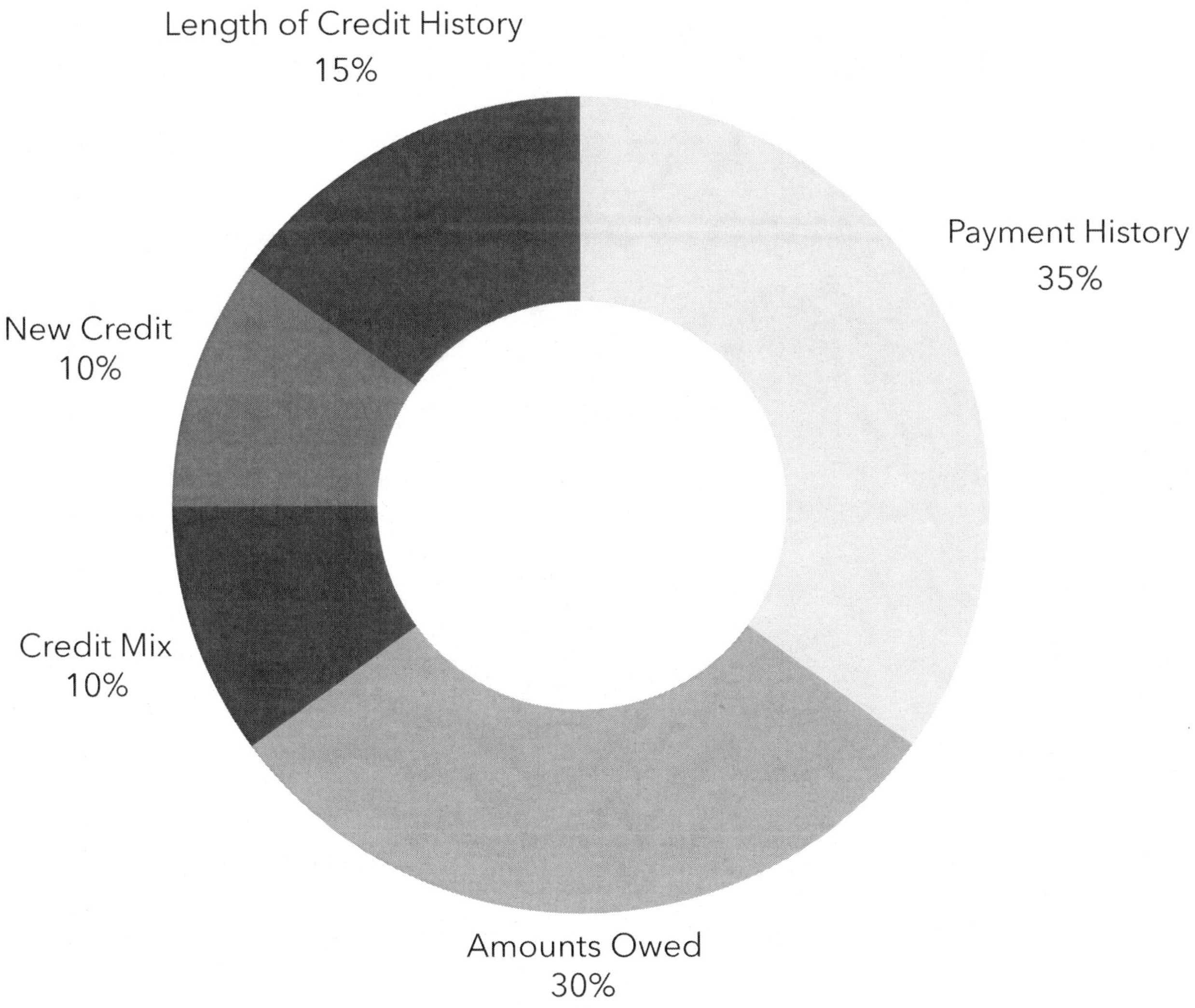

Payment History (35%) | 192.5 Points

- Record of on-time payments for credit accounts, such as credit cards, loans, and mortgages.
- Late payments, defaults, and bankruptcies negatively impact this factor.

Amounts Owed (30%) | 165 Points

- Total amount of debt owed compared to your available credit limits, known as credit utilization.
- High balances relative to your credit limit can lower your score.

Length of Credit History (15%) | 82 Points

- The length of time your credit accounts have been active.
- A longer credit history generally improves your score, as it shows more data on your borrowing habits.

Credit Mix (10%) | 55 Points

- The variety of credit types you have, such as credit cards, installment loans, mortgage loans, etc.
- A diverse mix of credit types can positively impact your score.

New Credit (10%) | 55 Points

- Recent applications for new credit and the number of new accounts opened.
- Frequent applications for new credit can lower your score temporarily due to hard inquiries.

What are the Credit Score Ranges?

Credit scores typically range from 300 to 850. Here's a breakdown of what different score ranges generally mean:

Poor (300-579)

- A poor credit score indicates significant credit risk and may result from late payments, defaults, or other negative credit events.
- Individuals with poor credit scores may have difficulty obtaining credit and, if approved, may face high interest rates and unfavorable terms.

Fair (580-669)

- A fair credit score shows moderate credit risk.
- Lenders may offer credit but with higher interest rates and less favorable terms

Good (670-739)

- A good credit score indicates lower credit risk.
- Borrowers are likely to be approved for credit with reasonable interest rates and terms.

Very Good (740-799)

- A very good credit score reflects a strong credit history and low credit risk.
- Individuals are likely to receive favorable loan terms and interest rates.

Excellent (800-850)

- An excellent credit score demonstrates minimal credit risk.
- Borrowers with excellent scores typically receive the best interest rates and credit terms.

Why Your Credit Score Matters

Your credit score affects various aspects of your financial life, including:

- **Loan Approval:** Lenders use your credit score to decide whether to approve your loan applications.
- **Interest Rates:** Higher scores typically qualify for lower interest rates, saving you money over time.
- **Credit Limits:** A good score can help you receive higher credit limits on credit cards and loans.
- **Rental Applications:** Landlords may check your credit score to determine your reliability as a tenant.
- **Employment Opportunities:** Some employers review credit scores as part of the hiring process, especially for jobs involving financial responsibility.

Tips for Maintaining and Building Good Credit

- **Make On-Time Payments:** Always pay at least the minimum payment by the due date. Late payments can significantly damage your credit score.

- **Keep Balances Low:** Aim to use less than 30% of your available credit limit to maintain a healthy credit utilization ratio.

- **Limit New Credit Applications:** Each new application results in a hard inquiry, which can temporarily lower your score. Apply for new credit only when necessary.

- **Diversify Your Credit Mix:** Having a mix of different types of credit (e.g., credit cards, installment loans) can positively impact your credit score.

- **Avoid Closing Old Accounts:** The length of your credit history matters, so keeping older accounts open can be beneficial, even if you don't use them regularly.

- **Monitor Your Credit Report:** Regularly check your credit report for errors and dispute any inaccuracies.

Understanding your credit score and how it's calculated can help you make informed financial decisions and improve your financial health.

How to Get Credit?

Getting credit involves establishing a credit history and demonstrating your ability to manage and repay borrowed money responsibly. Here are steps to help you get started and build good credit:

Open a Bank Account

While having a bank account itself doesn't build credit, it's a foundational step. A checking or savings account shows financial stability and responsibility.

Apply for a Secured Credit Card

A secured credit card is a great way to start building credit if you have no credit history. It requires a security deposit, which serves as your credit limit. Using the card responsibly and making on-time payments will help establish your credit history.

Become an Authorized User

Ask a family member or friend with good credit to add you as an authorized user on their credit card account. This allows you to benefit from their positive payment history and can boost your credit score.

Apply for a Credit-Builder Loan

Credit-builder loans are designed to help people build credit. The loan amount is held in a bank account while you make monthly payments. Once the loan is paid off, you get the money, and the lender reports your payment history to the credit bureaus.

Use a Cosigner

Credit-builder loans are designed to help people build credit. The loan amount is held in a bank account while you make monthly payments. Once the loan is paid off, you get the money, and the lender reports your payment history to the credit bureaus.

Retail Store Credit Cards

Retail store cards are often easier to qualify for than major credit cards. Use them sparingly and make sure to pay off the balance in full each month to avoid high interest rates.

Pay Bills on Time

While not all bill payments are reported to credit bureaus, consistently paying bills like rent, utilities, and phone bills on time can demonstrate financial responsibility. Some services, like Experian Boost, allow you to include utility and phone payments in your credit report.

Monitor Your Credit Report

Regularly check your credit report for errors or fraudulent activity. You can get a free credit report from each of the three major credit bureaus (Experian, Equifax, and TransUnion) once a year at AnnualCreditReport.com.

By following these steps and managing your credit responsibly, you can build a strong credit history that will open up more financial opportunities in the future.

Good vs. Bad Credit

Good Credit

Definition: Good credit typically refers to a credit score in the range of 670 to 799, with very good and excellent credit scores ranging from 740 to 850.

Characteristics:

- On-time payments: Consistently paying bills and loans on time.
- Low credit utilization: Keeping credit card balances low relative to credit limits.
- Long credit history: Having established credit accounts for a long period.
- Diverse credit mix: Managing different types of credit accounts responsibly.
- Minimal new credit inquiries: Avoiding frequent applications for new credit.

Bad Credit

Definition: Bad credit usually refers to a credit score below 580, with fair credit scores ranging from 580 to 669.

Characteristics:

- Late or missed payments: Frequently paying bills and loans late or not at all.
- High credit utilization: Using a large percentage of available credit.
- Short credit history: Limited credit accounts or recent establishment of credit.
- Limited credit mix: Having few or only one type of credit account.
- Multiple new credit inquiries: Applying for new credit frequently.

Impact of a Positive Credit Score

Loan and Credit Card Approvals

- Higher likelihood of approval for loans, mortgages, and credit cards.
- Access to higher credit limits and loan amounts.

Lower Interest Rates

- Qualification for lower interest rates on loans and credit cards, saving money on interest over time.

Better Loan Terms

- Access to more favorable loan terms, such as longer repayment periods and lower fees.

Rental Opportunities

- Easier approval for rental applications, as landlords prefer tenants with good credit.

Employment Opportunities

- Some employers check credit scores as part of the hiring process, particularly for roles involving financial responsibility.

Insurance Premiums

- Potentially lower premiums on auto and homeowners insurance, as some insurers use credit scores to determine rates.

Impact of a Negative Credit Score

Loan and Credit Card Denials

- Higher likelihood of being denied for loans, mortgages, and credit cards.
- Limited access to credit and lower credit limits if approved.

Higher Interest Rates

- Qualification for higher interest rates on loans and credit cards, increasing the cost of borrowing.

Unfavorable Loan Terms

- Access to less favorable loan terms, such as shorter repayment periods and higher fees.

Rental Challenges

- Difficulty in getting rental applications approved, as landlords may view bad credit as a sign of financial instability.

Employment Barriers

- Some employers may be hesitant to hire individuals with bad credit, particularly for positions involving financial management.

Higher Insurance Premiums

- Potentially higher premiums on auto and homeowners insurance, as insurers may view bad credit as a risk factor.

Increased Stress and Financial Strain

- Managing bad credit can lead to increased financial stress and limited access to financial resources during emergencies.

Tips for Improving a Negative Credit Score

- **Pay Bills on Time:** Ensure that all bills and loans are paid on time to establish a positive payment history.

- **Reduce Credit Card Balances:** Aim to lower credit utilization by paying down existing balances.

- **Avoid New Credit Applications:** Limit new credit inquiries to avoid further impact on your score.

- **Check Credit Reports Regularly:** Review credit reports for errors or inaccuracies and dispute them promptly.

- **Consider a Secured Credit Card:** Use a secured credit card to rebuild credit if you have a low score.

- **Seek Professional Help:** Consider working with a credit counseling service to create a plan for improving your credit.

Maintaining a good credit score is essential for financial health, providing access to better financial opportunities and reducing the cost of borrowing. If your credit score is currently low, taking steps to improve it can lead to significant benefits over time.

What is Credit Monitoring?

Credit monitoring is a service that tracks changes in your credit report and alerts you to any significant updates or suspicious activities. These services typically monitor your credit reports from the major credit bureaus–Experian, Equifax, and TransUnion–and notify you of changes such as:

- New accounts opened in your name
- Inquiries or applications for new credit
- Changes to your personal information (e.g., address changes)
- Late payments or delinquencies reported
- Public records such as bankruptcies or tax liens

Credit monitoring services can be provided for free or through paid subscriptions that offer more comprehensive coverage and additional features.

Why is Credit Monitoring Important?

Credit monitoring is a service that tracks changes in your credit report and alerts you to any significant updates or suspicious activities. These services typically monitor your credit reports from the major credit bureaus–Experian, Equifax, and TransUnion–and notify you of changes such as:

Early Detection of Identity Theft

- **Immediate Alerts:** Credit monitoring services notify you quickly if there are any unauthorized activities or suspicious changes to your credit report, allowing you to take prompt action.
- **Prevention:** Early detection can help prevent identity theft from escalating and causing significant financial harm.

Protection of Your Credit Score

- **Maintaining Good Credit:** By being aware of any negative changes or inaccuracies in your credit report, you can address them promptly to maintain a good credit score.
- **Dispute Errors:** If you notice errors in your credit report, credit monitoring services alert you to these issues so you can dispute them with the credit bureaus.

Financial Planning and Management

- **Stay Informed:** Regular updates on your credit status help you stay informed about your credit health, making it easier to plan for financial goals such as buying a home or car.
- **Credit Improvement:** Monitoring your credit can motivate you to make better financial decisions and improve your credit score over time.

Peace of Mind

- **Security:** Knowing that your credit is being monitored gives you peace of mind, as any significant changes will be reported to you promptly.
- **Proactive Measures:** With credit monitoring, you can take proactive measures to protect your financial health rather than reacting to problems after they have occurred.

Monitoring After a Data Breach

- **Increased Risk:** If your personal information has been exposed in a data breach, credit monitoring can help you keep an eye on your credit report for any fraudulent activities.
- **Mitigation:** Many companies offer free credit monitoring services to affected individuals after a data breach, helping mitigate the risk of identity theft.

Enhanced Features with Paid Services

- **Identity Theft Insurance:** Many paid credit monitoring services offer identity theft insurance, which can cover the costs associated with resolving identity theft.
- **Comprehensive Reports:** Paid services often provide more detailed credit reports and scores, as well as monitoring across all three major credit bureaus.
- **Additional Tools:** Some services offer financial tools and resources to help you manage your credit and finances more effectively.

Tips for Choosing a Credit Monitoring Service

- **Coverage:** Ensure the service monitors all three major credit bureaus – Experian, Equifax, and TransUnion.
- **Alerts:** Look for a service that provides real-time alerts for any significant changes to your credit report.
- **Identity Theft Protection:** Consider services that offer identity theft insurance and additional protection features.
- **Cost:** Compare free and paid options to determine which service best meets your needs and budget.
- **Reviews:** Read reviews and ratings of credit monitoring services to choose a reputable provider.

By using credit monitoring services, you can stay informed about your credit health, detect and prevent fraud, and take proactive steps to maintain or improve your credit score.

Credit Gem

Apply for a credit card when you turn 18 to start building credit.

Credit Gem

Productive Credit Profile

To build a well-rounded credit profile that covers all credit score categories, you should aim to have:

- 5 open primary accounts:
  - ☐ 3 active primary credit cards
  - ☐ 1 short-term installment loan
  - ☐ 1 long-term installment loan
- Credit utilization between 1-10%

"Your credit score doesn't define you, but a great one can open doors to fabulous opportunities!"

PART TWO

Understanding the Credit Report

What is a Credit Report?

A credit report is a detailed record of your credit history, maintained by credit bureaus. It includes information on your credit accounts, payment history, outstanding debts, and any public records like bankruptcies or tax liens. Lenders use this report to assess your creditworthiness when you apply for loans or credit.

Who Can Access Your Credit Information

- **You:** You have the right to access your own credit reports and credit score. You can obtain a free credit report from each of the three major credit bureaus (Equifax, Experian, and TransUnion) once a year through AnnualCreditReport.com.
- **Lenders and Creditors:** When you apply for credit, loans, or a rental agreement, lenders or creditors can access your credit report to assess your creditworthiness. They typically need your consent to perform this check.
- **Employers:** Potential employers may request a credit report as part of a background check, especially for positions that involve financial responsibilities. They must obtain your written permission before doing so.

- **Insurance Companies:** Insurance companies might check your credit report when you apply for insurance, especially for auto or homeowners insurance. They use this information to determine premiums and eligibility.
- **Landlords:** Landlords may review your credit history as part of the rental application process to evaluate your ability to pay rent.
- **Debt Collectors:** If you have delinquent debts, debt collectors may access your credit report to locate you and pursue collection efforts. They must follow regulations under the Fair Debt Collection Practices Act (FDCPA).

Who Cannot Access Your Credit Information

- **Unauthorized Individuals:** Friends, family, or acquaintances cannot access your credit score or history without your explicit permission.
- **Random Entities:** Entities or businesses cannot access your credit information without a permissible purpose, such as those related to credit, employment, or insurance.
- **Public Access:** Your credit information is not available to the general public and cannot be accessed through public records or social media.

Protecting Your Credit Information

- **Check Your Credit Reports Regularly:** Monitor your credit reports for any unauthorized activity or inaccuracies.
- **Use Strong Passwords:** Protect your online accounts with strong passwords and avoid sharing sensitive information.
- **Place Fraud Alerts:** If you suspect identity theft, you can place a fraud alert on your credit reports to make it harder for someone to open new accounts in your name.
- **Credit Freeze:** Consider placing a credit freeze to prevent new creditors from accessing your credit report without your authorization.

While certain parties may access your credit information with your consent or under specific conditions, unauthorized individuals cannot view your credit score or credit history without your permission.

What are Credit Inquiries?

Credit inquiries occur when someone checks your credit report. There are two types of inquiries:

Hard Inquiries

- Occur when a lender or creditor checks your credit report as part of a loan or credit card application process.
- Can affect your credit score and remain on your credit report for up to two years.

Soft Inquiries

- Occur when you check your own credit report, or when a lender checks your credit report for pre-approval offers.
- Do not affect your credit score.

Who are the Credit Bureaus?

The three major credit bureaus in the United States are:

- Equifax
- Experian
- TransUnion

How to Contact the Credit Bureaus?

Equifax

- Website: www.equifax.com
- Phone: 1-800-685-1111
- Mailing Address: Equifax Information Services LLC, P.O. Box 740256, Atlanta, GA 30374-0256

Experian

- Website: www.experian.com
- Phone: 1-888-397-3742
- Mailing Address: Experian, P.O. Box 4500, Allen, TX 75013

TransUnion

- Website: www.transunion.com
- Phone: 1-800-916-8800
- Mailing Address: TransUnion Consumer Solutions, P.O. Box 2000, Chester, PA 19016-2000

How to Access Your Credit Report?

You can access your credit report for free once a year from each of the three major credit bureaus through AnnualCreditReport.com. Here's how:

1. Visit AnnualCreditReport.com.
2. Fill out the form with your personal information.
3. Choose which credit bureau's report you want to access (Equifax, Experian, or TransUnion).
4. Answer the security questions to verify your identity.
5. Download or print your credit report.

How to Analyze Your Credit Report?

Check Personal Information

- Ensure your name, address, Social Security number, and other personal information are correct.

Review Credit Accounts

- Verify that all listed credit accounts are accurate and belong to you.
- Check the account status, payment history, and credit limits.

Look for Negative Information

- Identify any late payments, collections, charge-offs, or bankruptcies.
- Confirm that any negative information is accurate and within the reporting period.

Inspect Inquiries

- Review the list of hard and soft inquiries.
- Ensure that you recognize all hard inquiries.

Verify Public Records

- Check for any public records such as tax liens or judgments.
- Make sure they are accurate and belong to you.

How to File a Dispute?

If you find errors in your credit report, you can file a dispute with the credit bureaus.

Gather Documentation

- Collect any documents that support your dispute, such as bank statements, payment records, or letters from creditors.

Write a Dispute Letter

- Clearly identify the incorrect information.
- Provide a detailed explanation and include supporting documentation.
- Include your personal information and contact details.

Submit Your Dispute

- You can file a dispute online, by mail, or by phone with each credit bureau.

Equifax

- Online: Equifax Dispute
- Mail: Equifax Information Services LLC, P.O. Box 740256, Atlanta, GA 30374- 0256

Experian

- Online: Experian Dispute
- Mail: Experian, P.O. Box 4500, Allen, TX 75013

TransUnion

- Online: TransUnion Dispute
- Mail: TransUnion Consumer Solutions, P.O. Box 2000, Chester, PA 19016-2000

Dispute Checklist

1. Obtain Your Credit Report

- ☐ Obtain your credit reports from Equifax, Experian, and TransUnion
- ☐ Check for errors or inaccuracies in personal information, credit accounts, payment history, inquiries, and public records.

2. Review Your Credit Report

- ☐ Personal Information: Name, address, Social Security number, and date of birth.
- ☐ Credit Accounts: Incorrect account details, balances, or statuses.
- ☐ Negative Information: Late payments, collections, charge-offs, or bankruptcies.
- ☐ Inquiries: Unauthorized hard inquiries.
- ☐ Public Records: Tax liens, judgments, or bankruptcies.

3. Gather Supporting Documentation

- ☐ Collect documents that support your claim, such as:
    - ☐ Proof of Payment: Bank statements, payment confirmations.
    - ☐ Correspondence: Letters from creditors or collection agencies.
    - ☐ Account Statements: Credit card or loan statements showing correct information.
    - ☐ Legal Documents: Court records, if applicable.

4. Write a Dispute Letter

- [ ] Header: Include your name, address, phone number, and email.
- [ ] Date: The date of writing the letter.
- [ ] Credit Bureau Address: Include the address of the credit bureau where you are sending the dispute.
- [ ] Subject Line: "Credit Report Dispute"
- [ ] Introduction: Briefly state the purpose of the letter and mention the specific error(s) you are disputing.
- [ ] Details of the Dispute:
    - [ ] Clearly describe the error(s).
    - [ ] Provide a detailed explanation and include supporting documentation.
    - [ ] State the action you want (e.g., correction or removal of the disputed item).
- [ ] Attachments: Include copies of supporting documents.
- [ ] Signature: Sign the letter.

5. Submit Your Dispute

- Online
    - [ ] Equifax: Equifax Dispute
    - [ ] Experian: Experian Dispute
    - [ ] TransUnion: TransUnion Dispute
- By Mail
    - [ ] Equifax: Equifax Information Services LLC, P.O. Box 740256, Atlanta, GA 30374-0256
    - [ ] Experian: Experian, P.O. Box 4500, Allen, TX 75013
    - [ ] TransUnion: TransUnion Consumer Solutions, P.O. Box 2000, Chester, PA 19016-2000

- By Phone (less common):
  - [ ] Equifax: 1-800-685-1111
  - [ ] Experian: 1-888-397-3742
  - [ ] TransUnion: 1-800-916-8800

6. Keep Records

- [ ] Make copies of your dispute letter and any supporting documents.
- [ ] Save confirmation receipts from online disputes.
- [ ] Note down any reference numbers or case IDs provided.

7. Follow Up

- [ ] Monitor your credit report to ensure that the disputed information is corrected or removed.
- [ ] Check for updates from the credit bureau regarding the status of your dispute.

8. Review Updated Credit Report

- [ ] Obtain your updated credit reports from the credit bureaus to verify that the dispute has been resolved and the error corrected.

9. If Dispute is Not Resolved

- [ ] Request a Statement: Ask the credit bureau to include a statement of your dispute in your credit report.
- [ ] Escalate: Consider filing a complaint with the Consumer Financial Protection Bureau (CFPB) or seeking legal advice.

10. Monitor Your Credit Regularly

- [ ] Continue to check your credit reports periodically to catch any future inaccuracies or fraudulent activities early.

By following this checklist, you can effectively manage and resolve errors or inaccuracies on your credit report.

“Girls with good credit don't just shop for deals—they make them!”

PART THREE

Understanding Consumer Law

What is Consumer Law and How Does It Protect You?

Consumer law encompasses a range of legal protections designed to safeguard consumers in their interactions with businesses, especially regarding financial transactions and personal data. These laws are intended to prevent unfair practices, ensure transparency, and protect individuals' rights in the marketplace.

How Consumer Law Protects You

- **Prevents Unfair Practices:** Consumer laws protect against deceptive, fraudulent, and unfair practices by businesses.

- **Ensures Transparency:** Businesses must provide clear and accurate information about products and services.

- **Protects Privacy:** Laws regulate how businesses collect, use, and share personal information.

- **Provides Remedies:** If your rights are violated, consumer laws provide avenues for seeking redress and compensation.

- **Regulates Debt Collection:** Ensures that debt collectors adhere to ethical practices and protects consumers from harassment and abuse.

What is the Fair Credit Reporting Act (FCRA)?

The **Fair Credit Reporting Act (FCRA)** is a federal law designed to protect consumers by regulating the accuracy, fairness, and privacy of information in credit reports. Here's how the FCRA safeguards your rights:

1. Accuracy of Information:

- **Right to Accurate Information:** The FCRA mandates that credit reporting agencies (CRAs) maintain accurate and complete information. If you find errors or outdated information on your credit report, you have the right to dispute it, and the CRA must investigate and correct any inaccuracies.

2. Access to Your Credit Report:

- **Right to Access:** You have the right to request and obtain a copy of your credit report from each of the three major credit bureaus—Equifax, Experian, and TransUnion—once a year for free. This allows you to review your report for errors and ensure your credit history is accurate.

3. Fair Use of Your Credit Report:

- **Permissible Purposes:** The FCRA restricts who can access your credit report and under what circumstances. Only entities with a permissible purpose, such as lenders or employers with your consent, can request your credit report.

4. Consent for Access:

- **Authorization Required:** Before a lender or employer can access your credit report, they must obtain your written permission. This ensures that your credit information is only used with your consent and for legitimate purposes.

5. Notification of Negative Information:

- **Adverse Action Notice:** If a credit report is used to deny your application for credit, employment, or insurance, the FCRA requires the entity to provide you with an adverse action notice. This notice must include the name and contact information of the credit bureau that provided the report, as well as a summary of your rights.

6. Dispute Resolution:

- **Right to Dispute:** If you find inaccuracies on your credit report, you have the right to dispute them with the credit reporting agency. The agency must investigate your dispute, typically within 30 days, and correct any verified inaccuracies.

7. Limitations on Reporting Time:

- **Time Limits on Negative Information:** The FCRA limits how long negative information can remain on your credit report. For example, most negative information, such as late payments and collections, can only remain on your report for seven years, while bankruptcies can remain for up to ten years.

8. Protection of Privacy:

- **Confidentiality of Reports:** The FCRA protects your privacy by ensuring that your credit report is kept confidential and is only accessible to those who have a legitimate reason to review it. Unauthorized access or misuse of your credit information is prohibited.

9. Right to Correct Mistakes:

- **Correction of Errors:** If your credit report contains errors, you have the right to request corrections. The credit bureau must promptly address and rectify any verified inaccuracies, ensuring your credit report reflects accurate information.

The **Fair Credit Reporting Act (FCRA)** provides essential protections by ensuring the accuracy, fairness, and confidentiality of your credit information. It gives you the right to access and dispute errors on your credit report, limits who can access your information, and ensures that negative information is reported only within specific time frames. These protections help maintain the integrity of your credit report and safeguard your financial privacy.

What is the Fair Debt Collection Practices Act (FDCPA)?

The **Fair Debt Collection Practices Act (FDCPA)** is a federal law enacted to regulate the behavior of third-party debt collectors and protect consumers from abusive and deceptive practices. Here's how the FDCPA protects you:

1. Prevents Harassment and Abuse:

- **No Harassing Behavior:** Debt collectors are prohibited from using threatening or abusive language. This includes making threats of violence, using obscene or profane language, or repeatedly calling you at inconvenient times. These protections ensure that debt collectors cannot intimidate or distress you into paying.
- **Limits on Contact:** Debt collectors must adhere to reasonable contact hours (typically between 8 a.m. and 9 p.m.) and must stop contacting you if you request them to do so in writing. This helps prevent unwanted and intrusive communication.

2. Ensures Accurate Information:

- **Clear Disclosure:** Within five days of their initial contact with you, debt collectors must provide a written notice that includes the amount of the debt, the name of the creditor, and your rights to dispute the debt. This transparency helps you understand the debt and verify its legitimacy.

- **Prohibition of False Statements:** Debt collectors cannot misrepresent the amount or nature of the debt, nor can they falsely claim to be attorneys or government officials. This prevents misleading practices and ensures you receive accurate information.

3. Affords the Right to Dispute:

- **Debt Dispute and Verification:** If you dispute the debt in writing within 30 days of receiving the initial notice, the debt collector must cease collection activities until they provide verification of the debt. This allows you to challenge incorrect or disputed debts and ensures that only valid debts are pursued.

4. Protects Your Privacy:

- **Confidentiality:** Debt collectors cannot discuss your debt with third parties, such as friends, family, or neighbors, without your consent. This helps protect your privacy and prevents unnecessary embarrassment or intrusion into your personal life.

5. Provides the Option to Cease Communication:

- **Stop All Contact:** You have the right to request in writing that a debt collector stop all communication with you. Although they can still pursue legal action, they must respect your request to cease contact, helping you avoid unwanted interactions and stress.

6. Offers Legal Recourse:

- **Complaint Filing:** If a debt collector violates the FDCPA, you can file a complaint with the Consumer Financial Protection Bureau (CFPB) or your state's attorney general. This provides a formal channel for addressing grievances and seeking enforcement of your rights.
- **Suing for Damages:** You have the right to sue debt collectors in state or federal court for violations of the FDCPA. You may be entitled to damages for any harm caused, including emotional distress, and can also seek attorney's fees and court costs.

7. Regulates Collection Practices:

- **Fair Practices:** The FDCPA establishes clear guidelines for how debt collectors must conduct themselves, ensuring that they follow fair practices and do not engage in deceptive or manipulative tactics. This creates a more equitable process for debt collection and protects consumers from unfair treatment.

The FDCPA provides crucial protections by regulating the practices of debt collectors, ensuring fair treatment, and offering recourse if your rights are violated. It helps maintain a balance between creditors' rights to collect debts and consumers' rights to be treated with respect and dignity.

"Invest in your credit like you invest in your wardrobe—both will make you look and feel amazing."

PART FOUR

Understanding and Monitoring Your Monthly Financial Activities

- 52-Week Savings Challenge
- SMART Financial Goals Worksheet
- Credit Score Tracker
- Monthly Budget Planner
- Bills Payment Calendar
- Debt Repayment Plan
- Expense Tracker
- Credit Card Tracker
- Monthly Financial Reflection
- Wish List
- Emergency Fund Tracker
- Credit Networking and Mentorship
- Charity and Giving
- Self-Care and Financial Health

January

52-Week Money Saving *Challenge*

Goal Amount ____________

Week	Deposit	Balance	Done
1			☐
2			☐
3			☐
4			☐
5			☐
6			☐
7			☐
8			☐
9			☐
10			☐
11			☐
12			☐
13			☐
14			☐
15			☐
16			☐
17			☐
18			☐
19			☐
20			☐
21			☐
22			☐
23			☐
24			☐
25			☐
26			☐

Week	Deposit	Balance	Done
27			☐
28			☐
29			☐
30			☐
31			☐
32			☐
33			☐
34			☐
35			☐
36			☐
37			☐
38			☐
39			☐
40			☐
41			☐
42			☐
43			☐
44			☐
45			☐
46			☐
47			☐
48			☐
49			☐
50			☐
51			☐
52			☐

SMART Financial Goals *Worksheet*

JAN ○ FEB ○ MAR ○ APR ○ MAY ○ JUN ○ JUL ○ AUG ○ SEP ○ OCT ○ NOV ○ DEC ○

Description of Goals	SPECIFIC Cost	MEASURABLE Monthly Amount	ATTAINABLE Method/Steps	REALISTIC Goal Length	TIMEBOUND Your Timeline

Notes

Credit Score *Tracker*

JAN ○ FEB ○ MAR ○ APR ○ MAY ○ JUN ○ JUL ○ AUG ○ SEP ○ OCT ○ NOV ○ DEC ○

Current Score ________ **Goal Score** ________

900
850
800
750
700
650
600
550
500
450
400
350
300

WEEK 1 WEEK 2 WEEK 3 WEEK 4

Monthly Budget *Planner*

JAN ○ FEB ○ MAR ○ APR ○ MAY ○ JUN ○ JUL ○ AUG ○ SEP ○ OCT ○ NOV ○ DEC ○

INCOME	AMOUNT
TOTAL	

BILLS	AMOUNT
TOTAL	

SAVINGS	AMOUNT
TOTAL	

EXPENSES	AMOUNT
TOTAL	

DEBT	AMOUNT
TOTAL	

SUMMARY	AMOUNT
INCOME	
BILLS	
SAVINGS	
EXPENSES	
DEBTS	
TOTAL	

Bills Payment *Calendar*

JAN ○ FEB ○ MAR ○ APR ○ MAY ○ JUN ○ JUL ○ AUG ○ SEP ○ OCT ○ NOV ○ DEC ○

SUN	MON	TUE	WED	THU	FRI	SAT

Debt Repayment *Plan*

JAN ○ FEB ○ MAR ○ APR ○ MAY ○ JUN ○ JUL ○ AUG ○ SEP ○ OCT ○ NOV ○ DEC ○

Creditor ______________ Debt Type ______________

Starting Balance ______________ Credit Limit ______________

Repayment Frequency ______________ Interest Rate ______________

Goal Pay Off Date ______________ Min Repayment ______________

DATE	REPAYMENT	BALANCE	NOTES

Expense *Tracker*

JAN ○ FEB ○ MAR ○ APR ○ MAY ○ JUN ○ JUL ○ AUG ○ SEP ○ OCT ○ NOV ○ DEC ○

DATE	DESCRIPTION	AMOUNT	NOTES

TOTAL ______________

Credit Card *Tracker*

JAN ○ FEB ○ MAR ○ APR ○ MAY ○ JUN ○ JUL ○ AUG ○ SEP ○ OCT ○ NOV ○ DEC ○

DATE	CREDIT CARD	CREDIT LIMIT	% RATE	AMOUNT DUE	AMOUNT PAID	BALANCE

Monthly Financial *Reflection*

JAN ○ FEB ○ MAR ○ APR ○ MAY ○ JUN ○ JUL ○ AUG ○ SEP ○ OCT ○ NOV ○ DEC ○

TOTAL INCOME	TOTAL EXPENSES	DIFFERENCE	BALANCE

Biggest Wins this Month

What am I grateful for?

What do I need to improve for next month?

What did I learn by tracking my finances this month?

Wish List

JAN ○ FEB ○ MAR ○ APR ○ MAY ○ JUN ○ JUL ○ AUG ○ SEP ○ OCT ○ NOV ○ DEC ○

WISH LIST	HOPE TO PAY	WHERE TO BUY	BOUGHT	SPENT	SAVED	NOTES
			☐			
			☐			
			☐			
			☐			
			☐			
			☐			
			☐			
			☐			
			☐			
			☐			
			☐			
			☐			
			☐			
			☐			
			☐			
			☐			
			☐			
			☐			
			☐			
			☐			
			☐			
			☐			
			☐			
			☐			

Emergency Fund *Tracker*

JAN ○ FEB ○ MAR ○ APR ○ MAY ○ JUN ○ JUL ○ AUG ○ SEP ○ OCT ○ NOV ○ DEC ○

Amount Needed ______ Target Date ______

Monthly Savings Target ______ Account ______

Progress Tracker

10%	20%	30%	40%	50%	60%	70%	80%	90%	100%

DATE	DEPOSIT	WITHDRAW	NOTES	BALANCE

Notes

Credit Networking and *Mentorship*

JAN ○ FEB ○ MAR ○ APR ○ MAY ○ JUN ○ JUL ○ AUG ○ SEP ○ OCT ○ NOV ○ DEC ○

Networking Goals

What specific goals do you have for networking this month?

1 ____

2 ____

3 ____

Mentorship Goals

What do you want to achieve with the help of a mentor this month?

1 ____

2 ____

3 ____

Identify Networking Opportunities

Events & Workshops

List credit-related events, workshops, or webinars to attend this month:

1 ____

2 ____

3 ____

Online Communities

Identify online groups or forums where you can engage with others focused on credit improvement:

1 ______________________________

2 ______________________________

3 ______________________________

Track Your Progress

Networking Activities

Record your networking activities for the month (e.g., events attended, new connections made):

1 ______________________________

2 ______________________________

3 ______________________________

Mentorship Activities:

Record your interactions with mentors (e.g., meetings, advice received):

1 ______________________________

2 ______________________________

3 ______________________________

Notes

____

____

____

Charity and *Giving*

JAN ○ FEB ○ MAR ○ APR ○ MAY ○ JUN ○ JUL ○ AUG ○ SEP ○ OCT ○ NOV ○ DEC ○

DONATION	ORGANIZATION	DATE GIVEN	VALUE	TAX DEDUCTIBLE

Self-care and Financial *Health*

JAN ○ FEB ○ MAR ○ APR ○ MAY ○ JUN ○ JUL ○ AUG ○ SEP ○ OCT ○ NOV ○ DEC ○

Self-Care Reflection

- **Physical Well-being**

  What physical health activities will you focus on this month?

  - o ______________________________
  - o ______________________________

- **Emotional & Mental Wellness**

  What mental health activities will you focus on this month?

  - o ______________________________
  - o ______________________________

- **Time for Self-Care**

  How will you make time for yourself?

  - o ______________________________
  - o ______________________________

Financial Health Reflection

- **Current Financial Practices**

  What financial habits do you want to maintain or improve this month?

  - o ______________________________
  - o ______________________________

- **Financial Goals**

  List your financial goals for this month

  - ______________________________
  - ______________________________

- **Financial Self-Care**

  How will you manage financial stress?

  - ______________________________
  - ______________________________

Accountability & Progress

- **Support System**

  Who will help you stay accountable this month?

  - ______________________________
  - ______________________________

- **Tracking Progress**

  How will you monitor your progress? (e.g., weekly check-ins, journaling)

  - ______________________________
  - ______________________________

- **End-of-Month Review Date**

  Set a date to review your goals and make any necessary adjustments

  - ______________________________

February

SMART Financial Goals *Worksheet*

JAN ○ FEB ○ MAR ○ APR ○ MAY ○ JUN ○ JUL ○ AUG ○ SEP ○ OCT ○ NOV ○ DEC ○

Description of Goals	**SPECIFIC** Cost	**MEASURABLE** Monthly Amount	**ATTAINABLE** Method/Steps	**REALISTIC** Goal Length	**TIMEBOUND** Your Timeline

Notes

Credit Score *Tracker*

JAN ○ FEB ○ MAR ○ APR ○ MAY ○ JUN ○ JUL ○ AUG ○ SEP ○ OCT ○ NOV ○ DEC ○

Current Score ______ **Goal Score** ______

900
850
800
750
700
650
600
550
500
450
400
350
300

WEEK 1 WEEK 2 WEEK 3 WEEK 4

Monthly Budget *Planner*

JAN ○ FEB ○ MAR ○ APR ○ MAY ○ JUN ○ JUL ○ AUG ○ SEP ○ OCT ○ NOV ○ DEC ○

INCOME	AMOUNT
TOTAL	

BILLS	AMOUNT
TOTAL	

SAVINGS	AMOUNT
TOTAL	

EXPENSES	AMOUNT
TOTAL	

DEBT	AMOUNT
TOTAL	

SUMMARY	AMOUNT
INCOME	
BILLS	
SAVINGS	
EXPENSES	
DEBTS	
TOTAL	

Bills Payment *Calendar*

JAN ○ FEB ○ MAR ○ APR ○ MAY ○ JUN ○ JUL ○ AUG ○ SEP ○ OCT ○ NOV ○ DEC ○

SUN	MON	TUE	WED	THU	FRI	SAT

Debt Repayment *Plan*

JAN ○ FEB ○ MAR ○ APR ○ MAY ○ JUN ○ JUL ○ AUG ○ SEP ○ OCT ○ NOV ○ DEC ○

Creditor

Debt Type

Starting Balance

Credit Limit

Repayment Frequency

Interest Rate

Goal Pay Off Date

Min Repayment

DATE	REPAYMENT	BALANCE	NOTES

Expense *Tracker*

JAN ○ FEB ○ MAR ○ APR ○ MAY ○ JUN ○ JUL ○ AUG ○ SEP ○ OCT ○ NOV ○ DEC ○

DATE	DESCRIPTION	AMOUNT	NOTES

TOTAL ______________________

Credit Card *Tracker*

JAN	FEB	MAR	APR	MAY	JUN	JUL	AUG	SEP	OCT	NOV	DEC
○	○	○	○	○	○	○	○	○	○	○	○

DATE	CREDIT CARD	CREDIT LIMIT	% RATE	AMOUNT DUE	AMOUNT PAID	BALANCE

Monthly Financial *Reflection*

JAN ○ FEB ○ MAR ○ APR ○ MAY ○ JUN ○ JUL ○ AUG ○ SEP ○ OCT ○ NOV ○ DEC ○

TOTAL INCOME	TOTAL EXPENSES	DIFFERENCE	BALANCE

Biggest Wins this Month

____

____

____

____

What am I grateful for?

____

____

____

____

What do I need to improve for next month?

____

____

____

____

What did I learn by tracking my finances this month?

Wish *List*

JAN ○ FEB ○ MAR ○ APR ○ MAY ○ JUN ○ JUL ○ AUG ○ SEP ○ OCT ○ NOV ○ DEC ○

WISH LIST	HOPE TO PAY	WHERE TO BUY	BOUGHT	SPENT	SAVED	NOTES
			☐			
			☐			
			☐			
			☐			
			☐			
			☐			
			☐			
			☐			
			☐			
			☐			
			☐			
			☐			
			☐			
			☐			
			☐			
			☐			
			☐			
			☐			
			☐			
			☐			
			☐			
			☐			
			☐			
			☐			

Emergency Fund *Tracker*

JAN ○ FEB ○ MAR ○ APR ○ MAY ○ JUN ○ JUL ○ AUG ○ SEP ○ OCT ○ NOV ○ DEC ○

Amount Needed

Target Date

Monthly Savings Target

Account

Progress Tracker

10%	20%	30%	40%	50%	60%	70%	80%	90%	100%

DATE	DEPOSIT	WITHDRAW	NOTES	BALANCE

Notes

Credit Networking and *Mentorship*

JAN ○ FEB ○ MAR ○ APR ○ MAY ○ JUN ○ JUL ○ AUG ○ SEP ○ OCT ○ NOV ○ DEC ○

Networking Goals

What specific goals do you have for networking this month?

1 ______

2 ______

3 ______

Mentorship Goals

What do you want to achieve with the help of a mentor this month?

1 ______

2 ______

3 ______

Identify Networking Opportunities

Events & Workshops

List credit-related events, workshops, or webinars to attend this month:

1 ______

2 ______

3 ______

Online Communities

Identify online groups or forums where you can engage with others focused on credit improvement:

1 ______________________________

2 ______________________________

3 ______________________________

Track Your Progress

Networking Activities

Record your networking activities for the month (e.g., events attended, new connections made):

1 ______________________________

2 ______________________________

3 ______________________________

Mentorship Activities:

Record your interactions with mentors (e.g., meetings, advice received):

1 ______________________________

2 ______________________________

3 ______________________________

Notes

____

____

____

Charity and *Giving*

JAN ○ FEB ○ MAR ○ APR ○ MAY ○ JUN ○ JUL ○ AUG ○ SEP ○ OCT ○ NOV ○ DEC ○

DONATION	ORGANIZATION	DATE GIVEN	VALUE	TAX DEDUCTIBLE

Self-care and Financial *Health*

JAN ○ FEB ○ MAR ○ APR ○ MAY ○ JUN ○ JUL ○ AUG ○ SEP ○ OCT ○ NOV ○ DEC ○

Self-Care Reflection

- **Physical Well-being**

  What physical health activities will you focus on this month?

  o ______________________________

  o ______________________________

- **Emotional & Mental Wellness**

  What mental health activities will you focus on this month?

  o ______________________________

  o ______________________________

- **Time for Self-Care**

  How will you make time for yourself?

  o ______________________________

  o ______________________________

Financial Health Reflection

- **Current Financial Practices**

  What financial habits do you want to maintain or improve this month?

  o ______________________________

  o ______________________________

- **Financial Goals**

  List your financial goals for this month

  - ________________________________
  - ________________________________

- **Financial Self-Care**

  How will you manage financial stress?

  - ________________________________
  - ________________________________

Accountability & Progress

- **Support System**

  Who will help you stay accountable this month?

  - ________________________________
  - ________________________________

- **Tracking Progress**

  How will you monitor your progress? (e.g., weekly check-ins, journaling)

  - ________________________________
  - ________________________________

- **End-of-Month Review Date**

  Set a date to review your goals and make any necessary adjustments

  - ________________________________

March

SMART Financial Goals *Worksheet*

JAN ○ FEB ○ MAR ○ APR ○ MAY ○ JUN ○ JUL ○ AUG ○ SEP ○ OCT ○ NOV ○ DEC ○

Description of Goals	**SPECIFIC** Cost	**MEASURABLE** Monthly Amount	**ATTAINABLE** Method/Steps	**REALISTIC** Goal Length	**TIMEBOUND** Your Timeline

Notes

Credit Score *Tracker*

JAN ○ FEB ○ MAR ○ APR ○ MAY ○ JUN ○ JUL ○ AUG ○ SEP ○ OCT ○ NOV ○ DEC ○

Current Score ______________ **Goal Score** ______________

900
850
800
750
700
650
600
550
500
450
400
350
300

WEEK 1 WEEK 2 WEEK 3 WEEK 4

Monthly Budget *Planner*

JAN ○ FEB ○ MAR ○ APR ○ MAY ○ JUN ○ JUL ○ AUG ○ SEP ○ OCT ○ NOV ○ DEC ○

INCOME	AMOUNT
TOTAL	

BILLS	AMOUNT
TOTAL	

SAVINGS	AMOUNT
TOTAL	

EXPENSES	AMOUNT
TOTAL	

DEBT	AMOUNT
TOTAL	

SUMMARY	AMOUNT
INCOME	
BILLS	
SAVINGS	
EXPENSES	
DEBTS	
TOTAL	

Bills Payment *Calendar*

JAN ○ FEB ○ MAR ○ APR ○ MAY ○ JUN ○ JUL ○ AUG ○ SEP ○ OCT ○ NOV ○ DEC ○

SUN	MON	TUE	WED	THU	FRI	SAT

Debt Repayment *Plan*

JAN ○ FEB ○ MAR ○ APR ○ MAY ○ JUN ○ JUL ○ AUG ○ SEP ○ OCT ○ NOV ○ DEC ○

Creditor

Debt Type

Starting Balance

Credit Limit

Repayment Frequency

Interest Rate

Goal Pay Off Date

Min Repayment

DATE	REPAYMENT	BALANCE	NOTES

Expense *Tracker*

JAN ○ FEB ○ MAR ○ APR ○ MAY ○ JUN ○ JUL ○ AUG ○ SEP ○ OCT ○ NOV ○ DEC ○

DATE	DESCRIPTION	AMOUNT	NOTES

TOTAL ______________________

Credit Card *Tracker*

JAN ○ FEB ○ MAR ○ APR ○ MAY ○ JUN ○ JUL ○ AUG ○ SEP ○ OCT ○ NOV ○ DEC ○

DATE	CREDIT CARD	CREDIT LIMIT	% RATE	AMOUNT DUE	AMOUNT PAID	BALANCE

Monthly Financial *Reflection*

JAN ○ FEB ○ MAR ○ APR ○ MAY ○ JUN ○ JUL ○ AUG ○ SEP ○ OCT ○ NOV ○ DEC ○

TOTAL INCOME	TOTAL EXPENSES	DIFFERENCE	BALANCE

Biggest Wins this Month

What am I grateful for?

What do I need to improve for next month?

What did I learn by tracking my finances this month?

Wish *List*

JAN	FEB	MAR	APR	MAY	JUN	JUL	AUG	SEP	OCT	NOV	DEC
○	○	○	○	○	○	○	○	○	○	○	○

WISH LIST	HOPE TO PAY	WHERE TO BUY	BOUGHT	SPENT	SAVED	NOTES
			☐			
			☐			
			☐			
			☐			
			☐			
			☐			
			☐			
			☐			
			☐			
			☐			
			☐			
			☐			
			☐			
			☐			
			☐			
			☐			
			☐			
			☐			
			☐			
			☐			
			☐			
			☐			
			☐			
			☐			

Emergency Fund Tracker

JAN ○ FEB ○ MAR ○ APR ○ MAY ○ JUN ○ JUL ○ AUG ○ SEP ○ OCT ○ NOV ○ DEC ○

Amount Needed ______ Target Date ______

Monthly Savings Target ______ Account ______

Progress Tracker

10%	20%	30%	40%	50%	60%	70%	80%	90%	100%

DATE	DEPOSIT	WITHDRAW	NOTES	BALANCE

Notes

Credit Networking and *Mentorship*

JAN ○ FEB ○ MAR ○ APR ○ MAY ○ JUN ○ JUL ○ AUG ○ SEP ○ OCT ○ NOV ○ DEC ○

Networking Goals

What specific goals do you have for networking this month?

1 ______________________________

2 ______________________________

3 ______________________________

Mentorship Goals

What do you want to achieve with the help of a mentor this month?

1 ______________________________

2 ______________________________

3 ______________________________

Identify Networking Opportunities

Events & Workshops

List credit-related events, workshops, or webinars to attend this month:

1 ______________________________

2 ______________________________

3 ______________________________

Online Communities

Identify online groups or forums where you can engage with others focused on credit improvement:

1 ______________________________

2 ______________________________

3 ______________________________

Track Your Progress

Networking Activities

Record your networking activities for the month (e.g., events attended, new connections made):

1 ______________________________

2 ______________________________

3 ______________________________

Mentorship Activities:

Record your interactions with mentors (e.g., meetings, advice received):

1 ______________________________

2 ______________________________

3 ______________________________

Notes

____

____

____

Charity and *Giving*

JAN ○ FEB ○ MAR ○ APR ○ MAY ○ JUN ○ JUL ○ AUG ○ SEP ○ OCT ○ NOV ○ DEC ○

DONATION	ORGANIZATION	DATE GIVEN	VALUE	TAX DEDUCTIBLE

Self-care and Financial *Health*

JAN ○ FEB ○ MAR ○ APR ○ MAY ○ JUN ○ JUL ○ AUG ○ SEP ○ OCT ○ NOV ○ DEC ○

Self-Care Reflection

- **Physical Well-being**

  What physical health activities will you focus on this month?

  o ____

  o ____

- **Emotional & Mental Wellness**

  What mental health activities will you focus on this month?

  o ____

  o ____

- **Time for Self-Care**

  How will you make time for yourself?

  o ____

  o ____

Financial Health Reflection

- **Current Financial Practices**

  What financial habits do you want to maintain or improve this month?

  o ____

  o ____

- **Financial Goals**

  List your financial goals for this month

  - ______________________________
  - ______________________________

- **Financial Self-Care**

  How will you manage financial stress?

  - ______________________________
  - ______________________________

Accountability & Progress

- **Support System**

  Who will help you stay accountable this month?

  - ______________________________
  - ______________________________

- **Tracking Progress**

  How will you monitor your progress? (e.g., weekly check-ins, journaling)

  - ______________________________
  - ______________________________

- **End-of-Month Review Date**

  Set a date to review your goals and make any necessary adjustments

  - ______________________________

April

SMART Financial Goals *Worksheet*

JAN ○ FEB ○ MAR ○ APR ○ MAY ○ JUN ○ JUL ○ AUG ○ SEP ○ OCT ○ NOV ○ DEC ○

Description of Goals	**SPECIFIC** Cost	**MEASURABLE** Monthly Amount	**ATTAINABLE** Method/Steps	**REALISTIC** Goal Length	**TIMEBOUND** Your Timeline

Notes

Credit Score *Tracker*

JAN ○ FEB ○ MAR ○ APR ○ MAY ○ JUN ○ JUL ○ AUG ○ SEP ○ OCT ○ NOV ○ DEC ○

Current Score ______________ **Goal Score** ______________

900
850
800
750
700
650
600
550
500
450
400
350
300

WEEK 1 WEEK 2 WEEK 3 WEEK 4

Monthly Budget *Planner*

JAN ○ FEB ○ MAR ○ APR ○ MAY ○ JUN ○ JUL ○ AUG ○ SEP ○ OCT ○ NOV ○ DEC ○

INCOME	AMOUNT
TOTAL	

BILLS	AMOUNT
TOTAL	

SAVINGS	AMOUNT
TOTAL	

EXPENSES	AMOUNT
TOTAL	

DEBT	AMOUNT
TOTAL	

SUMMARY	AMOUNT
INCOME	
BILLS	
SAVINGS	
EXPENSES	
DEBTS	
TOTAL	

Bills Payment *Calendar*

JAN ○ FEB ○ MAR ○ APR ○ MAY ○ JUN ○ JUL ○ AUG ○ SEP ○ OCT ○ NOV ○ DEC ○

SUN	MON	TUE	WED	THU	FRI	SAT

Debt Repayment *Plan*

JAN ○ FEB ○ MAR ○ APR ○ MAY ○ JUN ○ JUL ○ AUG ○ SEP ○ OCT ○ NOV ○ DEC ○

Creditor ______ Debt Type ______

Starting Balance ______ Credit Limit ______

Repayment Frequency ______ Interest Rate ______

Goal Pay Off Date ______ Min Repayment ______

DATE	REPAYMENT	BALANCE	NOTES

Expense *Tracker*

JAN ○ FEB ○ MAR ○ APR ○ MAY ○ JUN ○ JUL ○ AUG ○ SEP ○ OCT ○ NOV ○ DEC ○

DATE	DESCRIPTION	AMOUNT	NOTES

TOTAL ______________________

Credit Card *Tracker*

JAN ○ FEB ○ MAR ○ APR ○ MAY ○ JUN ○ JUL ○ AUG ○ SEP ○ OCT ○ NOV ○ DEC ○

DATE	CREDIT CARD	CREDIT LIMIT	% RATE	AMOUNT DUE	AMOUNT PAID	BALANCE

Monthly Financial *Reflection*

JAN ○ FEB ○ MAR ○ APR ○ MAY ○ JUN ○ JUL ○ AUG ○ SEP ○ OCT ○ NOV ○ DEC ○

TOTAL INCOME	TOTAL EXPENSES	DIFFERENCE	BALANCE

Biggest Wins this Month

What am I grateful for?

What do I need to improve for next month?

What did I learn by tracking my finances this month?

Wish *List*

JAN ○ FEB ○ MAR ○ APR ○ MAY ○ JUN ○ JUL ○ AUG ○ SEP ○ OCT ○ NOV ○ DEC ○

WISH LIST	HOPE TO PAY	WHERE TO BUY	BOUGHT	SPENT	SAVED	NOTES
			☐			
			☐			
			☐			
			☐			
			☐			
			☐			
			☐			
			☐			
			☐			
			☐			
			☐			
			☐			
			☐			
			☐			
			☐			
			☐			
			☐			
			☐			
			☐			
			☐			
			☐			
			☐			
			☐			
			☐			

Emergency Fund *Tracker*

JAN ○ FEB ○ MAR ○ APR ○ MAY ○ JUN ○ JUL ○ AUG ○ SEP ○ OCT ○ NOV ○ DEC ○

Amount Needed

Target Date

Monthly Savings Target

Account

Progress Tracker

10%	20%	30%	40%	50%	60%	70%	80%	90%	100%

DATE	DEPOSIT	WITHDRAW	NOTES	BALANCE

Notes

Credit Networking and *Mentorship*

JAN ○ FEB ○ MAR ○ APR ○ MAY ○ JUN ○ JUL ○ AUG ○ SEP ○ OCT ○ NOV ○ DEC ○

Networking Goals

What specific goals do you have for networking this month?

1 ____

2 ____

3 ____

Mentorship Goals

What do you want to achieve with the help of a mentor this month?

1 ____

2 ____

3 ____

Identify Networking Opportunities

Events & Workshops

List credit-related events, workshops, or webinars to attend this month:

1 ____

2 ____

3 ____

Online Communities

Identify online groups or forums where you can engage with others focused on credit improvement:

1 ______________________________

2 ______________________________

3 ______________________________

Track Your Progress

Networking Activities

Record your networking activities for the month (e.g., events attended, new connections made):

1 ______________________________

2 ______________________________

3 ______________________________

Mentorship Activities:

Record your interactions with mentors (e.g., meetings, advice received):

1 ______________________________

2 ______________________________

3 ______________________________

Notes

____

____

____

Charity and *Giving*

JAN ○ FEB ○ MAR ○ APR ○ MAY ○ JUN ○ JUL ○ AUG ○ SEP ○ OCT ○ NOV ○ DEC ○

DONATION	ORGANIZATION	DATE GIVEN	VALUE	TAX DEDUCTIBLE

Self-care and Financial *Health*

JAN ○ FEB ○ MAR ○ APR ○ MAY ○ JUN ○ JUL ○ AUG ○ SEP ○ OCT ○ NOV ○ DEC ○

Self-Care Reflection

- **Physical Well-being**

  What physical health activities will you focus on this month?

  o ______________________________

  o ______________________________

- **Emotional & Mental Wellness**

  What mental health activities will you focus on this month?

  o ______________________________

  o ______________________________

- **Time for Self-Care**

  How will you make time for yourself?

  o ______________________________

  o ______________________________

Financial Health Reflection

- **Current Financial Practices**

  What financial habits do you want to maintain or improve this month?

  o ______________________________

  o ______________________________

- **Financial Goals**

  List your financial goals for this month

  - o ______________________________
  - o ______________________________

- **Financial Self-Care**

  How will you manage financial stress?

  - o ______________________________
  - o ______________________________

Accountability & Progress

- **Support System**

  Who will help you stay accountable this month?

  - o ______________________________
  - o ______________________________

- **Tracking Progress**

  How will you monitor your progress? (e.g., weekly check-ins, journaling)

  - o ______________________________
  - o ______________________________

- **End-of-Month Review Date**

  Set a date to review your goals and make any necessary adjustments

  - o ______________________________

May

SMART Financial Goals *Worksheet*

JAN ○ FEB ○ MAR ○ APR ○ MAY ○ JUN ○ JUL ○ AUG ○ SEP ○ OCT ○ NOV ○ DEC ○

Description of Goals	**SPECIFIC** Cost	**MEASURABLE** Monthly Amount	**ATTAINABLE** Method/Steps	**REALISTIC** Goal Length	**TIMEBOUND** Your Timeline

Notes

Credit Score *Tracker*

JAN ○ FEB ○ MAR ○ APR ○ MAY ○ JUN ○ JUL ○ AUG ○ SEP ○ OCT ○ NOV ○ DEC ○

Current Score ______ **Goal Score** ______

900

850

800

750

700

650

600

550

500

450

400

350

300

WEEK 1 WEEK 2 WEEK 3 WEEK 4

Monthly Budget *Planner*

JAN ○ FEB ○ MAR ○ APR ○ MAY ○ JUN ○ JUL ○ AUG ○ SEP ○ OCT ○ NOV ○ DEC ○

INCOME	AMOUNT
TOTAL	

BILLS	AMOUNT
TOTAL	

SAVINGS	AMOUNT
TOTAL	

EXPENSES	AMOUNT
TOTAL	

DEBT	AMOUNT
TOTAL	

SUMMARY	AMOUNT
INCOME	
BILLS	
SAVINGS	
EXPENSES	
DEBTS	
TOTAL	

Bills Payment *Calendar*

JAN ○ FEB ○ MAR ○ APR ○ MAY ○ JUN ○ JUL ○ AUG ○ SEP ○ OCT ○ NOV ○ DEC ○

SUN	MON	TUE	WED	THU	FRI	SAT

Debt Repayment *Plan*

JAN ○ FEB ○ MAR ○ APR ○ MAY ○ JUN ○ JUL ○ AUG ○ SEP ○ OCT ○ NOV ○ DEC ○

Creditor

Debt Type

Starting Balance

Credit Limit

Repayment Frequency

Interest Rate

Goal Pay Off Date

Min Repayment

DATE	REPAYMENT	BALANCE	NOTES

Expense *Tracker*

JAN ○ FEB ○ MAR ○ APR ○ MAY ○ JUN ○ JUL ○ AUG ○ SEP ○ OCT ○ NOV ○ DEC ○

DATE	DESCRIPTION	AMOUNT	NOTES

TOTAL ______________________

Credit Card *Tracker*

JAN ○ FEB ○ MAR ○ APR ○ MAY ○ JUN ○ JUL ○ AUG ○ SEP ○ OCT ○ NOV ○ DEC ○

DATE	CREDIT CARD	CREDIT LIMIT	% RATE	AMOUNT DUE	AMOUNT PAID	BALANCE

Monthly Financial *Reflection*

JAN ○ FEB ○ MAR ○ APR ○ MAY ○ JUN ○ JUL ○ AUG ○ SEP ○ OCT ○ NOV ○ DEC ○

TOTAL INCOME	TOTAL EXPENSES	DIFFERENCE	BALANCE

Biggest Wins this Month

____

____

____

____

What am I grateful for?

____

____

____

____

What do I need to improve for next month?

____

____

____

____

What did I learn by tracking my finances this month?

Wish *List*

JAN ○ FEB ○ MAR ○ APR ○ MAY ○ JUN ○ JUL ○ AUG ○ SEP ○ OCT ○ NOV ○ DEC ○

WISH LIST	HOPE TO PAY	WHERE TO BUY	BOUGHT	SPENT	SAVED	NOTES
			☐			
			☐			
			☐			
			☐			
			☐			
			☐			
			☐			
			☐			
			☐			
			☐			
			☐			
			☐			
			☐			
			☐			
			☐			
			☐			
			☐			
			☐			
			☐			
			☐			
			☐			
			☐			
			☐			
			☐			

Emergency Fund Tracker

JAN	FEB	MAR	APR	MAY	JUN	JUL	AUG	SEP	OCT	NOV	DEC
○	○	○	○	○	○	○	○	○	○	○	○

Amount Needed

Target Date

Monthly Savings Target

Account

Progress Tracker

10%	20%	30%	40%	50%	60%	70%	80%	90%	100%

DATE	DEPOSIT	WITHDRAW	NOTES	BALANCE

Notes

Credit Networking and *Mentorship*

JAN ○ FEB ○ MAR ○ APR ○ MAY ○ JUN ○ JUL ○ AUG ○ SEP ○ OCT ○ NOV ○ DEC ○

Networking Goals

What specific goals do you have for networking this month?

1 ____________________

2 ____________________

3 ____________________

Mentorship Goals

What do you want to achieve with the help of a mentor this month?

1 ____________________

2 ____________________

3 ____________________

Identify Networking Opportunities

Events & Workshops

List credit-related events, workshops, or webinars to attend this month:

1 ____________________

2 ____________________

3 ____________________

Online Communities

Identify online groups or forums where you can engage with others focused on credit improvement:

1 ______________________________

2 ______________________________

3 ______________________________

Track Your Progress

Networking Activities

Record your networking activities for the month (e.g., events attended, new connections made):

1 ______________________________

2 ______________________________

3 ______________________________

Mentorship Activities:

Record your interactions with mentors (e.g., meetings, advice received):

1 ______________________________

2 ______________________________

3 ______________________________

Notes

____

____

____

Charity and *Giving*

JAN ○ FEB ○ MAR ○ APR ○ MAY ○ JUN ○ JUL ○ AUG ○ SEP ○ OCT ○ NOV ○ DEC ○

DONATION	ORGANIZATION	DATE GIVEN	VALUE	TAX DEDUCTIBLE

Self-care and Financial *Health*

JAN ○ FEB ○ MAR ○ APR ○ MAY ○ JUN ○ JUL ○ AUG ○ SEP ○ OCT ○ NOV ○ DEC ○

Self-Care Reflection

- **Physical Well-being**

  What physical health activities will you focus on this month?

  - ____________________
  - ____________________

- **Emotional & Mental Wellness**

  What mental health activities will you focus on this month?

  - ____________________
  - ____________________

- **Time for Self-Care**

  How will you make time for yourself?

  - ____________________
  - ____________________

Financial Health Reflection

- **Current Financial Practices**

  What financial habits do you want to maintain or improve this month?

  - ____________________
  - ____________________

- **Financial Goals**

  List your financial goals for this month

  - ________________________________
  - ________________________________

- **Financial Self-Care**

  How will you manage financial stress?

  - ________________________________
  - ________________________________

Accountability & Progress

- **Support System**

  Who will help you stay accountable this month?

  - ________________________________
  - ________________________________

- **Tracking Progress**

  How will you monitor your progress? (e.g., weekly check-ins, journaling)

  - ________________________________
  - ________________________________

- **End-of-Month Review Date**

  Set a date to review your goals and make any necessary adjustments

  - ________________________________

June

SMART Financial Goals *Worksheet*

JAN ○ FEB ○ MAR ○ APR ○ MAY ○ JUN ○ JUL ○ AUG ○ SEP ○ OCT ○ NOV ○ DEC ○

Description of Goals	**SPECIFIC** Cost	**MEASURABLE** Monthly Amount	**ATTAINABLE** Method/Steps	**REALISTIC** Goal Length	**TIMEBOUND** Your Timeline

Notes

Credit Score *Tracker*

JAN ○ FEB ○ MAR ○ APR ○ MAY ○ JUN ○ JUL ○ AUG ○ SEP ○ OCT ○ NOV ○ DEC ○

Current Score ______ **Goal Score** ______

900
850
800
750
700
650
600
550
500
450
400
350
300

WEEK 1 WEEK 2 WEEK 3 WEEK 4

Monthly Budget *Planner*

JAN ○ FEB ○ MAR ○ APR ○ MAY ○ JUN ○ JUL ○ AUG ○ SEP ○ OCT ○ NOV ○ DEC ○

INCOME	AMOUNT
TOTAL	

BILLS	AMOUNT
TOTAL	

SAVINGS	AMOUNT
TOTAL	

EXPENSES	AMOUNT
TOTAL	

DEBT	AMOUNT
TOTAL	

SUMMARY	AMOUNT
INCOME BILLS	
SAVINGS	
EXPENSES	
DEBTS	
TOTAL	

Bills Payment *Calendar*

JAN ○ FEB ○ MAR ○ APR ○ MAY ○ JUN ○ JUL ○ AUG ○ SEP ○ OCT ○ NOV ○ DEC ○

SUN	MON	TUE	WED	THU	FRI	SAT

Debt Repayment *Plan*

JAN ○ FEB ○ MAR ○ APR ○ MAY ○ JUN ○ JUL ○ AUG ○ SEP ○ OCT ○ NOV ○ DEC ○

Creditor

Debt Type

Starting Balance

Credit Limit

Repayment Frequency

Interest Rate

Goal Pay Off Date

Min Repayment

DATE	REPAYMENT	BALANCE	NOTES

Expense *Tracker*

JAN ○ FEB ○ MAR ○ APR ○ MAY ○ JUN ○ JUL ○ AUG ○ SEP ○ OCT ○ NOV ○ DEC ○

DATE	DESCRIPTION	AMOUNT	NOTES

TOTAL ____________________

Credit Card *Tracker*

JAN ○ FEB ○ MAR ○ APR ○ MAY ○ JUN ○ JUL ○ AUG ○ SEP ○ OCT ○ NOV ○ DEC ○

DATE	CREDIT CARD	CREDIT LIMIT	% RATE	AMOUNT DUE	AMOUNT PAID	BALANCE

Monthly Financial *Reflection*

JAN ○ FEB ○ MAR ○ APR ○ MAY ○ JUN ○ JUL ○ AUG ○ SEP ○ OCT ○ NOV ○ DEC ○

TOTAL INCOME	TOTAL EXPENSES	DIFFERENCE	BALANCE

Biggest Wins this Month

What am I grateful for?

What do I need to improve for next month?

What did I learn by tracking my finances this month?

Wish *List*

JAN ○ FEB ○ MAR ○ APR ○ MAY ○ JUN ○ JUL ○ AUG ○ SEP ○ OCT ○ NOV ○ DEC ○

WISH LIST	HOPE TO PAY	WHERE TO BUY	BOUGHT	SPENT	SAVED	NOTES
			☐			
			☐			
			☐			
			☐			
			☐			
			☐			
			☐			
			☐			
			☐			
			☐			
			☐			
			☐			
			☐			
			☐			
			☐			
			☐			
			☐			
			☐			
			☐			
			☐			
			☐			
			☐			
			☐			
			☐			

Emergency Fund *Tracker*

JAN ○ FEB ○ MAR ○ APR ○ MAY ○ JUN ○ JUL ○ AUG ○ SEP ○ OCT ○ NOV ○ DEC ○

Amount Needed

Target Date

Monthly Savings Target

Account

Progress Tracker

10%	20%	30%	40%	50%	60%	70%	80%	90%	100%

DATE	DEPOSIT	WITHDRAW	NOTES	BALANCE

Notes

Credit Networking and *Mentorship*

JAN ○ FEB ○ MAR ○ APR ○ MAY ○ JUN ○ JUL ○ AUG ○ SEP ○ OCT ○ NOV ○ DEC ○

Networking Goals

What specific goals do you have for networking this month?

1 ____________________

2 ____________________

3 ____________________

Mentorship Goals

What do you want to achieve with the help of a mentor this month?

1 ____________________

2 ____________________

3 ____________________

Identify Networking Opportunities

Events & Workshops

List credit-related events, workshops, or webinars to attend this month:

1 ____________________

2 ____________________

3 ____________________

Online Communities

Identify online groups or forums where you can engage with others focused on credit improvement:

1 ______________________________

2 ______________________________

3 ______________________________

Track Your Progress

Networking Activities

Record your networking activities for the month (e.g., events attended, new connections made):

1 ______________________________

2 ______________________________

3 ______________________________

Mentorship Activities:

Record your interactions with mentors (e.g., meetings, advice received):

1 ______________________________

2 ______________________________

3 ______________________________

Notes

____

____

____

Charity and *Giving*

JAN	FEB	MAR	APR	MAY	JUN	JUL	AUG	SEP	OCT	NOV	DEC
○	○	○	○	○	○	○	○	○	○	○	○

DONATION	ORGANIZATION	DATE GIVEN	VALUE	TAX DEDUCTIBLE

Self-care and Financial *Health*

JAN ○ FEB ○ MAR ○ APR ○ MAY ○ JUN ○ JUL ○ AUG ○ SEP ○ OCT ○ NOV ○ DEC ○

Self-Care Reflection

- **Physical Well-being**

  What physical health activities will you focus on this month?

  - o ______
  - o ______

- **Emotional & Mental Wellness**

  What mental health activities will you focus on this month?

  - o ______
  - o ______

- **Time for Self-Care**

  How will you make time for yourself?

  - o ______
  - o ______

Financial Health Reflection

- **Current Financial Practices**

  What financial habits do you want to maintain or improve this month?

  - o ______
  - o ______

- **Financial Goals**

  List your financial goals for this month

  - ______________________________
  - ______________________________

- **Financial Self-Care**

  How will you manage financial stress?

  - ______________________________
  - ______________________________

Accountability & Progress

- **Support System**

  Who will help you stay accountable this month?

  - ______________________________
  - ______________________________

- **Tracking Progress**

  How will you monitor your progress? (e.g., weekly check-ins, journaling)

  - ______________________________
  - ______________________________

- **End-of-Month Review Date**

  Set a date to review your goals and make any necessary adjustments

  - ______________________________

July

SMART Financial Goals *Worksheet*

JAN ○ FEB ○ MAR ○ APR ○ MAY ○ JUN ○ JUL ○ AUG ○ SEP ○ OCT ○ NOV ○ DEC ○

Description of Goals	**SPECIFIC** Cost	**MEASURABLE** Monthly Amount	**ATTAINABLE** Method/Steps	**REALISTIC** Goal Length	**TIMEBOUND** Your Timeline

Notes

Credit Score *Tracker*

JAN ○ FEB ○ MAR ○ APR ○ MAY ○ JUN ○ JUL ○ AUG ○ SEP ○ OCT ○ NOV ○ DEC ○

Current Score ______ **Goal Score** ______

900
850
800
750
700
650
600
550
500
450
400
350
300

WEEK 1 WEEK 2 WEEK 3 WEEK 4

Monthly Budget *Planner*

JAN ○ FEB ○ MAR ○ APR ○ MAY ○ JUN ○ JUL ○ AUG ○ SEP ○ OCT ○ NOV ○ DEC ○

INCOME	AMOUNT
TOTAL	

BILLS	AMOUNT
TOTAL	

SAVINGS	AMOUNT
TOTAL	

EXPENSES	AMOUNT
TOTAL	

DEBT	AMOUNT
TOTAL	

SUMMARY	AMOUNT
INCOME	
BILLS	
SAVINGS	
EXPENSES	
DEBTS	
TOTAL	

Bills Payment *Calendar*

JAN ○ FEB ○ MAR ○ APR ○ MAY ○ JUN ○ JUL ○ AUG ○ SEP ○ OCT ○ NOV ○ DEC ○

SUN	MON	TUE	WED	THU	FRI	SAT

Debt Repayment *Plan*

JAN ○ FEB ○ MAR ○ APR ○ MAY ○ JUN ○ JUL ○ AUG ○ SEP ○ OCT ○ NOV ○ DEC ○

Creditor ____________________ Debt Type ____________________

Starting Balance ____________________ Credit Limit ____________________

Repayment Frequency ____________________ Interest Rate ____________________

Goal Pay Off Date ____________________ Min Repayment ____________________

DATE	REPAYMENT	BALANCE	NOTES

Expense *Tracker*

JAN ○ FEB ○ MAR ○ APR ○ MAY ○ JUN ○ JUL ○ AUG ○ SEP ○ OCT ○ NOV ○ DEC ○

DATE	DESCRIPTION	AMOUNT	NOTES

TOTAL ____________________

Credit Card *Tracker*

JAN ○ FEB ○ MAR ○ APR ○ MAY ○ JUN ○ JUL ○ AUG ○ SEP ○ OCT ○ NOV ○ DEC ○

DATE	CREDIT CARD	CREDIT LIMIT	% RATE	AMOUNT DUE	AMOUNT PAID	BALANCE

Monthly Financial *Reflection*

JAN ○ FEB ○ MAR ○ APR ○ MAY ○ JUN ○ JUL ○ AUG ○ SEP ○ OCT ○ NOV ○ DEC ○

TOTAL INCOME	TOTAL EXPENSES	DIFFERENCE	BALANCE

Biggest Wins this Month

What am I grateful for?

What do I need to improve for next month?

What did I learn by tracking my finances this month?

Wish *List*

JAN ○ FEB ○ MAR ○ APR ○ MAY ○ JUN ○ JUL ○ AUG ○ SEP ○ OCT ○ NOV ○ DEC ○

WISH LIST	HOPE TO PAY	WHERE TO BUY	BOUGHT	SPENT	SAVED	NOTES
			☐			
			☐			
			☐			
			☐			
			☐			
			☐			
			☐			
			☐			
			☐			
			☐			
			☐			
			☐			
			☐			
			☐			
			☐			
			☐			
			☐			
			☐			
			☐			
			☐			
			☐			
			☐			
			☐			
			☐			

Emergency Fund *Tracker*

JAN ○ FEB ○ MAR ○ APR ○ MAY ○ JUN ○ JUL ○ AUG ○ SEP ○ OCT ○ NOV ○ DEC ○

Amount Needed ______ Target Date ______

Monthly Savings Target ______ Account ______

Progress Tracker

10%	20%	30%	40%	50%	60%	70%	80%	90%	100%

DATE	DEPOSIT	WITHDRAW	NOTES	BALANCE

Notes

Credit Networking and *Mentorship*

JAN ○ FEB ○ MAR ○ APR ○ MAY ○ JUN ○ JUL ○ AUG ○ SEP ○ OCT ○ NOV ○ DEC ○

Networking Goals

What specific goals do you have for networking this month?

1 ______________________

2 ______________________

3 ______________________

Mentorship Goals

What do you want to achieve with the help of a mentor this month?

1 ______________________

2 ______________________

3 ______________________

Identify Networking Opportunities

Events & Workshops

List credit-related events, workshops, or webinars to attend this month:

1 ______________________

2 ______________________

3 ______________________

Online Communities

Identify online groups or forums where you can engage with others focused on credit improvement:

1 ____

2 ____

3 ____

Track Your Progress

Networking Activities

Record your networking activities for the month (e.g., events attended, new connections made):

1 ____

2 ____

3 ____

Mentorship Activities:

Record your interactions with mentors (e.g., meetings, advice received):

1 ____

2 ____

3 ____

Notes

____

____

____

Charity and *Giving*

JAN ○ FEB ○ MAR ○ APR ○ MAY ○ JUN ○ JUL ○ AUG ○ SEP ○ OCT ○ NOV ○ DEC ○

DONATION	ORGANIZATION	DATE GIVEN	VALUE	TAX DEDUCTIBLE

Self-care and Financial *Health*

JAN ○ FEB ○ MAR ○ APR ○ MAY ○ JUN ○ JUL ○ AUG ○ SEP ○ OCT ○ NOV ○ DEC ○

Self-Care Reflection

- **Physical Well-being**

  What physical health activities will you focus on this month?

  - o ______________________________
  - o ______________________________

- **Emotional & Mental Wellness**

  What mental health activities will you focus on this month?

  - o ______________________________
  - o ______________________________

- **Time for Self-Care**

  How will you make time for yourself?

  - o ______________________________
  - o ______________________________

Financial Health Reflection

- **Current Financial Practices**

  What financial habits do you want to maintain or improve this month?

  - o ______________________________
  - o ______________________________

- **Financial Goals**

  List your financial goals for this month

  o ______________________________

  o ______________________________

- **Financial Self-Care**

  How will you manage financial stress?

  o ______________________________

  o ______________________________

Accountability & Progress

- **Support System**

  Who will help you stay accountable this month?

  o ______________________________

  o ______________________________

- **Tracking Progress**

  How will you monitor your progress? (e.g., weekly check-ins, journaling)

  o ______________________________

  o ______________________________

- **End-of-Month Review Date**

  Set a date to review your goals and make any necessary adjustments

  o ______________________________

August

SMART Financial Goals *Worksheet*

JAN ○ FEB ○ MAR ○ APR ○ MAY ○ JUN ○ JUL ○ AUG ○ SEP ○ OCT ○ NOV ○ DEC ○

Description of Goals	SPECIFIC Cost	MEASURABLE Monthly Amount	ATTAINABLE Method/Steps	REALISTIC Goal Length	TIMEBOUND Your Timeline

Notes

Credit Score *Tracker*

JAN ○ FEB ○ MAR ○ APR ○ MAY ○ JUN ○ JUL ○ AUG ○ SEP ○ OCT ○ NOV ○ DEC ○

Current Score ______ **Goal Score** ______

900
850
800
750
700
650
600
550
500
450
400
350
300

WEEK 1 WEEK 2 WEEK 3 WEEK 4

Monthly Budget *Planner*

JAN ○ FEB ○ MAR ○ APR ○ MAY ○ JUN ○ JUL ○ AUG ○ SEP ○ OCT ○ NOV ○ DEC ○

INCOME	AMOUNT
TOTAL	

BILLS	AMOUNT
TOTAL	

SAVINGS	AMOUNT
TOTAL	

EXPENSES	AMOUNT
TOTAL	

DEBT	AMOUNT
TOTAL	

SUMMARY	AMOUNT
INCOME	
BILLS	
SAVINGS	
EXPENSES	
DEBTS	
TOTAL	

Bills Payment *Calendar*

JAN ○ FEB ○ MAR ○ APR ○ MAY ○ JUN ○ JUL ○ AUG ○ SEP ○ OCT ○ NOV ○ DEC ○

SUN	MON	TUE	WED	THU	FRI	SAT

Debt Repayment *Plan*

JAN ○ FEB ○ MAR ○ APR ○ MAY ○ JUN ○ JUL ○ AUG ○ SEP ○ OCT ○ NOV ○ DEC ○

Creditor ____________ Debt Type ____________

Starting Balance ____________ Credit Limit ____________

Repayment Frequency ____________ Interest Rate ____________

Goal Pay Off Date ____________ Min Repayment ____________

DATE	REPAYMENT	BALANCE	NOTES

Expense *Tracker*

JAN ○ FEB ○ MAR ○ APR ○ MAY ○ JUN ○ JUL ○ AUG ○ SEP ○ OCT ○ NOV ○ DEC ○

DATE	DESCRIPTION	AMOUNT	NOTES

TOTAL ______________________

Credit Card *Tracker*

JAN ○ FEB ○ MAR ○ APR ○ MAY ○ JUN ○ JUL ○ AUG ○ SEP ○ OCT ○ NOV ○ DEC ○

DATE	CREDIT CARD	CREDIT LIMIT	% RATE	AMOUNT DUE	AMOUNT PAID	BALANCE

Monthly Financial *Reflection*

JAN ○ FEB ○ MAR ○ APR ○ MAY ○ JUN ○ JUL ○ AUG ○ SEP ○ OCT ○ NOV ○ DEC ○

TOTAL INCOME	TOTAL EXPENSES	DIFFERENCE	BALANCE

Biggest Wins this Month

What am I grateful for?

What do I need to improve for next month?

What did I learn by tracking my finances this month?

Wish *List*

JAN ○ FEB ○ MAR ○ APR ○ MAY ○ JUN ○ JUL ○ AUG ○ SEP ○ OCT ○ NOV ○ DEC ○

WISH LIST	HOPE TO PAY	WHERE TO BUY	BOUGHT	SPENT	SAVED	NOTES
			☐			
			☐			
			☐			
			☐			
			☐			
			☐			
			☐			
			☐			
			☐			
			☐			
			☐			
			☐			
			☐			
			☐			
			☐			
			☐			
			☐			
			☐			
			☐			
			☐			
			☐			
			☐			
			☐			
			☐			

Emergency Fund *Tracker*

JAN ○ FEB ○ MAR ○ APR ○ MAY ○ JUN ○ JUL ○ AUG ○ SEP ○ OCT ○ NOV ○ DEC ○

Amount Needed

Target Date

Monthly Savings Target

Account

Progress Tracker

10%	20%	30%	40%	50%	60%	70%	80%	90%	100%

DATE	DEPOSIT	WITHDRAW	NOTES	BALANCE

Notes

Credit Networking and *Mentorship*

JAN ○ FEB ○ MAR ○ APR ○ MAY ○ JUN ○ JUL ○ AUG ○ SEP ○ OCT ○ NOV ○ DEC ○

Networking Goals

What specific goals do you have for networking this month?

1 ____________________

2 ____________________

3 ____________________

Mentorship Goals

What do you want to achieve with the help of a mentor this month?

1 ____________________

2 ____________________

3 ____________________

Identify Networking Opportunities

Events & Workshops

List credit-related events, workshops, or webinars to attend this month:

1 ____________________

2 ____________________

3 ____________________

Online Communities

Identify online groups or forums where you can engage with others focused on credit improvement:

1 ____________________

2 ____________________

3 ____________________

Track Your Progress

Networking Activities

Record your networking activities for the month (e.g., events attended, new connections made):

1 ____________________

2 ____________________

3 ____________________

Mentorship Activities:

Record your interactions with mentors (e.g., meetings, advice received):

1 ____________________

2 ____________________

3 ____________________

Notes

Charity and *Giving*

JAN ○ FEB ○ MAR ○ APR ○ MAY ○ JUN ○ JUL ○ AUG ○ SEP ○ OCT ○ NOV ○ DEC ○

DONATION	ORGANIZATION	DATE GIVEN	VALUE	TAX DEDUCTIBLE

Self-care and Financial *Health*

JAN ○ FEB ○ MAR ○ APR ○ MAY ○ JUN ○ JUL ○ AUG ○ SEP ○ OCT ○ NOV ○ DEC ○

Self-Care Reflection

- **Physical Well-being**

  What physical health activities will you focus on this month?

  ○ ______________________________

  ○ ______________________________

- **Emotional & Mental Wellness**

  What mental health activities will you focus on this month?

  ○ ______________________________

  ○ ______________________________

- **Time for Self-Care**

  How will you make time for yourself?

  ○ ______________________________

  ○ ______________________________

Financial Health Reflection

- **Current Financial Practices**

  What financial habits do you want to maintain or improve this month?

  ○ ______________________________

  ○ ______________________________

- **Financial Goals**

  List your financial goals for this month

  - ______________________________
  - ______________________________

- **Financial Self-Care**

  How will you manage financial stress?

  - ______________________________
  - ______________________________

Accountability & Progress

- **Support System**

  Who will help you stay accountable this month?

  - ______________________________
  - ______________________________

- **Tracking Progress**

  How will you monitor your progress? (e.g., weekly check-ins, journaling)

  - ______________________________
  - ______________________________

- **End-of-Month Review Date**

  Set a date to review your goals and make any necessary adjustments

  - ______________________________

September

SMART Financial Goals *Worksheet*

JAN ○ FEB ○ MAR ○ APR ○ MAY ○ JUN ○ JUL ○ AUG ○ SEP ○ OCT ○ NOV ○ DEC ○

Description of Goals	**SPECIFIC** Cost	**MEASURABLE** Monthly Amount	**ATTAINABLE** Method/Steps	**REALISTIC** Goal Length	**TIMEBOUND** Your Timeline

Notes

Credit Score *Tracker*

JAN ○ FEB ○ MAR ○ APR ○ MAY ○ JUN ○ JUL ○ AUG ○ SEP ○ OCT ○ NOV ○ DEC ○

Current Score ______ **Goal Score** ______

900
850
800
750
700
650
600
550
500
450
400
350
300

WEEK 1 WEEK 2 WEEK 3 WEEK 4

Monthly Budget *Planner*

JAN ○ FEB ○ MAR ○ APR ○ MAY ○ JUN ○ JUL ○ AUG ○ SEP ○ OCT ○ NOV ○ DEC ○

INCOME	AMOUNT
TOTAL	

BILLS	AMOUNT
TOTAL	

SAVINGS	AMOUNT
TOTAL	

EXPENSES	AMOUNT
TOTAL	

DEBT	AMOUNT
TOTAL	

SUMMARY	AMOUNT
INCOME	
BILLS	
SAVINGS	
EXPENSES	
DEBTS	
TOTAL	

Bills Payment *Calendar*

JAN ○ FEB ○ MAR ○ APR ○ MAY ○ JUN ○ JUL ○ AUG ○ SEP ○ OCT ○ NOV ○ DEC ○

SUN	MON	TUE	WED	THU	FRI	SAT

Debt Repayment *Plan*

JAN ○ FEB ○ MAR ○ APR ○ MAY ○ JUN ○ JUL ○ AUG ○ SEP ○ OCT ○ NOV ○ DEC ○

Creditor

Debt Type

Starting Balance

Credit Limit

Repayment Frequency

Interest Rate

Goal Pay Off Date

Min Repayment

DATE	REPAYMENT	BALANCE	NOTES

Expense *Tracker*

JAN ○ FEB ○ MAR ○ APR ○ MAY ○ JUN ○ JUL ○ AUG ○ SEP ○ OCT ○ NOV ○ DEC ○

DATE	DESCRIPTION	AMOUNT	NOTES

TOTAL ______________________

Credit Card *Tracker*

JAN ○ FEB ○ MAR ○ APR ○ MAY ○ JUN ○ JUL ○ AUG ○ SEP ○ OCT ○ NOV ○ DEC ○

DATE	CREDIT CARD	CREDIT LIMIT	% RATE	AMOUNT DUE	AMOUNT PAID	BALANCE

Monthly Financial *Reflection*

JAN ○ FEB ○ MAR ○ APR ○ MAY ○ JUN ○ JUL ○ AUG ○ SEP ○ OCT ○ NOV ○ DEC ○

TOTAL INCOME	TOTAL EXPENSES	DIFFERENCE	BALANCE

Biggest Wins this Month

What am I grateful for?

What do I need to improve for next month?

What did I learn by tracking my finances this month?

Wish *List*

JAN ○ FEB ○ MAR ○ APR ○ MAY ○ JUN ○ JUL ○ AUG ○ SEP ○ OCT ○ NOV ○ DEC ○

WISH LIST	HOPE TO PAY	WHERE TO BUY	BOUGHT	SPENT	SAVED	NOTES
			☐			
			☐			
			☐			
			☐			
			☐			
			☐			
			☐			
			☐			
			☐			
			☐			
			☐			
			☐			
			☐			
			☐			
			☐			
			☐			
			☐			
			☐			
			☐			
			☐			
			☐			
			☐			
			☐			
			☐			

Emergency Fund *Tracker*

JAN ○ FEB ○ MAR ○ APR ○ MAY ○ JUN ○ JUL ○ AUG ○ SEP ○ OCT ○ NOV ○ DEC ○

Amount Needed ______ Target Date ______

Monthly Savings Target ______ Account ______

Progress Tracker

10%	20%	30%	40%	50%	60%	70%	80%	90%	100%

DATE	DEPOSIT	WITHDRAW	NOTES	BALANCE

Notes

Credit Networking and *Mentorship*

JAN ○ FEB ○ MAR ○ APR ○ MAY ○ JUN ○ JUL ○ AUG ○ SEP ○ OCT ○ NOV ○ DEC ○

Networking Goals

What specific goals do you have for networking this month?

1 ______________________________

2 ______________________________

3 ______________________________

Mentorship Goals

What do you want to achieve with the help of a mentor this month?

1 ______________________________

2 ______________________________

3 ______________________________

Identify Networking Opportunities

Events & Workshops

List credit-related events, workshops, or webinars to attend this month:

1 ______________________________

2 ______________________________

3 ______________________________

Online Communities

Identify online groups or forums where you can engage with others focused on credit improvement:

1 ______________________________

2 ______________________________

3 ______________________________

Track Your Progress

Networking Activities

Record your networking activities for the month (e.g., events attended, new connections made):

1 ______________________________

2 ______________________________

3 ______________________________

Mentorship Activities:

Record your interactions with mentors (e.g., meetings, advice received):

1 ______________________________

2 ______________________________

3 ______________________________

Notes

____

____

____

Charity and *Giving*

JAN ○ FEB ○ MAR ○ APR ○ MAY ○ JUN ○ JUL ○ AUG ○ SEP ○ OCT ○ NOV ○ DEC ○

DONATION	ORGANIZATION	DATE GIVEN	VALUE	TAX DEDUCTIBLE

Self-care and Financial *Health*

JAN FEB MAR APR MAY JUN JUL AUG SEP OCT NOV DEC

○ ○ ○ ○ ○ ○ ○ ○ ○ ○ ○ ○

Self-Care Reflection

- **Physical Well-being**

  What physical health activities will you focus on this month?

  - o ____
  - o ____

- **Emotional & Mental Wellness**

  What mental health activities will you focus on this month?

  - o ____
  - o ____

- **Time for Self-Care**

  How will you make time for yourself?

  - o ____
  - o ____

Financial Health Reflection

- **Current Financial Practices**

  What financial habits do you want to maintain or improve this month?

  - o ____
  - o ____

- **Financial Goals**

  List your financial goals for this month

  - ______________________________
  - ______________________________

- **Financial Self-Care**

  How will you manage financial stress?

  - ______________________________
  - ______________________________

Accountability & Progress

- **Support System**

  Who will help you stay accountable this month?

  - ______________________________
  - ______________________________

- **Tracking Progress**

  How will you monitor your progress? (e.g., weekly check-ins, journaling)

  - ______________________________
  - ______________________________

- **End-of-Month Review Date**

  Set a date to review your goals and make any necessary adjustments

  - ______________________________

October

SMART Financial Goals *Worksheet*

JAN ○ FEB ○ MAR ○ APR ○ MAY ○ JUN ○ JUL ○ AUG ○ SEP ○ OCT ○ NOV ○ DEC ○

Description of Goals	**SPECIFIC** Cost	**MEASURABLE** Monthly Amount	**ATTAINABLE** Method/Steps	**REALISTIC** Goal Length	**TIMEBOUND** Your Timeline

Notes

Credit Score *Tracker*

JAN ○ FEB ○ MAR ○ APR ○ MAY ○ JUN ○ JUL ○ AUG ○ SEP ○ OCT ○ NOV ○ DEC ○

Current Score ____________ **Goal Score** ____________

900
850
800
750
700
650
600
550
500
450
400
350
300

WEEK 1 WEEK 2 WEEK 3 WEEK 4

Monthly Budget *Planner*

JAN ○ FEB ○ MAR ○ APR ○ MAY ○ JUN ○ JUL ○ AUG ○ SEP ○ OCT ○ NOV ○ DEC ○

INCOME	AMOUNT
TOTAL	

BILLS	AMOUNT
TOTAL	

SAVINGS	AMOUNT
TOTAL	

EXPENSES	AMOUNT
TOTAL	

DEBT	AMOUNT
TOTAL	

SUMMARY	AMOUNT
INCOME	
BILLS	
SAVINGS	
EXPENSES	
DEBTS	
TOTAL	

Bills Payment *Calendar*

JAN ○ FEB ○ MAR ○ APR ○ MAY ○ JUN ○ JUL ○ AUG ○ SEP ○ OCT ○ NOV ○ DEC ○

SUN	MON	TUE	WED	THU	FRI	SAT

Debt Repayment *Plan*

JAN ○ FEB ○ MAR ○ APR ○ MAY ○ JUN ○ JUL ○ AUG ○ SEP ○ OCT ○ NOV ○ DEC ○

Creditor

Debt Type

Starting Balance

Credit Limit

Repayment Frequency

Interest Rate

Goal Pay Off Date

Min Repayment

DATE	REPAYMENT	BALANCE	NOTES

Expense *Tracker*

JAN ○ FEB ○ MAR ○ APR ○ MAY ○ JUN ○ JUL ○ AUG ○ SEP ○ OCT ○ NOV ○ DEC ○

DATE	DESCRIPTION	AMOUNT	NOTES

TOTAL ______________________

Credit Card *Tracker*

JAN ○ FEB ○ MAR ○ APR ○ MAY ○ JUN ○ JUL ○ AUG ○ SEP ○ OCT ○ NOV ○ DEC ○

DATE	CREDIT CARD	CREDIT LIMIT	% RATE	AMOUNT DUE	AMOUNT PAID	BALANCE

Monthly Financial *Reflection*

JAN ○ FEB ○ MAR ○ APR ○ MAY ○ JUN ○ JUL ○ AUG ○ SEP ○ OCT ○ NOV ○ DEC ○

TOTAL INCOME	TOTAL EXPENSES	DIFFERENCE	BALANCE

Biggest Wins this Month

What am I grateful for?

What do I need to improve for next month?

What did I learn by tracking my finances this month?

Wish *List*

JAN	FEB	MAR	APR	MAY	JUN	JUL	AUG	SEP	OCT	NOV	DEC
○	○	○	○	○	○	○	○	○	○	○	○

WISH LIST	HOPE TO PAY	WHERE TO BUY	BOUGHT	SPENT	SAVED	NOTES
			☐			
			☐			
			☐			
			☐			
			☐			
			☐			
			☐			
			☐			
			☐			
			☐			
			☐			
			☐			
			☐			
			☐			
			☐			
			☐			
			☐			
			☐			
			☐			
			☐			
			☐			
			☐			
			☐			
			☐			

Emergency Fund *Tracker*

JAN ○ FEB ○ MAR ○ APR ○ MAY ○ JUN ○ JUL ○ AUG ○ SEP ○ OCT ○ NOV ○ DEC ○

Amount Needed ______ Target Date ______

Monthly Savings Target ______ Account ______

Progress Tracker

10%	20%	30%	40%	50%	60%	70%	80%	90%	100%

DATE	DEPOSIT	WITHDRAW	NOTES	BALANCE

Notes

Credit Networking and *Mentorship*

JAN ○ FEB ○ MAR ○ APR ○ MAY ○ JUN ○ JUL ○ AUG ○ SEP ○ OCT ○ NOV ○ DEC ○

Networking Goals

What specific goals do you have for networking this month?

1 ______________________________

2 ______________________________

3 ______________________________

Mentorship Goals

What do you want to achieve with the help of a mentor this month?

1 ______________________________

2 ______________________________

3 ______________________________

Identify Networking Opportunities

Events & Workshops

List credit-related events, workshops, or webinars to attend this month:

1 ______________________________

2 ______________________________

3 ______________________________

Online Communities

Identify online groups or forums where you can engage with others focused on credit improvement:

1 ______________________________

2 ______________________________

3 ______________________________

Track Your Progress

Networking Activities

Record your networking activities for the month (e.g., events attended, new connections made):

1 ______________________________

2 ______________________________

3 ______________________________

Mentorship Activities:

Record your interactions with mentors (e.g., meetings, advice received):

1 ______________________________

2 ______________________________

3 ______________________________

Notes

____

____

____

Charity and *Giving*

JAN ○ FEB ○ MAR ○ APR ○ MAY ○ JUN ○ JUL ○ AUG ○ SEP ○ OCT ○ NOV ○ DEC ○

DONATION	ORGANIZATION	DATE GIVEN	VALUE	TAX DEDUCTIBLE

Self-care and Financial *Health*

JAN ○ FEB ○ MAR ○ APR ○ MAY ○ JUN ○ JUL ○ AUG ○ SEP ○ OCT ○ NOV ○ DEC ○

Self-Care Reflection

- **Physical Well-being**

  What physical health activities will you focus on this month?

  - ○ ____________________
  - ○ ____________________

- **Emotional & Mental Wellness**

  What mental health activities will you focus on this month?

  - ○ ____________________
  - ○ ____________________

- **Time for Self-Care**

  How will you make time for yourself?

  - ○ ____________________
  - ○ ____________________

Financial Health Reflection

- **Current Financial Practices**

  What financial habits do you want to maintain or improve this month?

  - ○ ____________________
  - ○ ____________________

- **Financial Goals**

  List your financial goals for this month

  - ______________________
  - ______________________

- **Financial Self-Care**

  How will you manage financial stress?

  - ______________________
  - ______________________

Accountability & Progress

- **Support System**

  Who will help you stay accountable this month?

  - ______________________
  - ______________________

- **Tracking Progress**

  How will you monitor your progress? (e.g., weekly check-ins, journaling)

  - ______________________
  - ______________________

- **End-of-Month Review Date**

  Set a date to review your goals and make any necessary adjustments

  - ______________________

November

SMART Financial Goals *Worksheet*

JAN ○ FEB ○ MAR ○ APR ○ MAY ○ JUN ○ JUL ○ AUG ○ SEP ○ OCT ○ NOV ○ DEC ○

Description of Goals	**SPECIFIC** Cost	**MEASURABLE** Monthly Amount	**ATTAINABLE** Method/Steps	**REALISTIC** Goal Length	**TIMEBOUND** Your Timeline

Notes

Credit Score *Tracker*

JAN ○ FEB ○ MAR ○ APR ○ MAY ○ JUN ○ JUL ○ AUG ○ SEP ○ OCT ○ NOV ○ DEC ○

Current Score ________ **Goal Score** ________

900
850
800
750
700
650
600
550
500
450
400
350
300

WEEK 1 WEEK 2 WEEK 3 WEEK 4

Monthly Budget *Planner*

JAN ○ FEB ○ MAR ○ APR ○ MAY ○ JUN ○ JUL ○ AUG ○ SEP ○ OCT ○ NOV ○ DEC ○

INCOME	AMOUNT
TOTAL	

BILLS	AMOUNT
TOTAL	

SAVINGS	AMOUNT
TOTAL	

EXPENSES	AMOUNT
TOTAL	

DEBT	AMOUNT
TOTAL	

SUMMARY	AMOUNT
INCOME	
BILLS	
SAVINGS	
EXPENSES	
DEBTS	
TOTAL	

Bills Payment *Calendar*

JAN ○ FEB ○ MAR ○ APR ○ MAY ○ JUN ○ JUL ○ AUG ○ SEP ○ OCT ○ NOV ○ DEC ○

SUN	MON	TUE	WED	THU	FRI	SAT

Debt Repayment *Plan*

JAN ○ FEB ○ MAR ○ APR ○ MAY ○ JUN ○ JUL ○ AUG ○ SEP ○ OCT ○ NOV ○ DEC ○

Creditor

Debt Type

Starting Balance

Credit Limit

Repayment Frequency

Interest Rate

Goal Pay Off Date

Min Repayment

DATE	REPAYMENT	BALANCE	NOTES

Expense *Tracker*

JAN ○ FEB ○ MAR ○ APR ○ MAY ○ JUN ○ JUL ○ AUG ○ SEP ○ OCT ○ NOV ○ DEC ○

DATE	DESCRIPTION	AMOUNT	NOTES

TOTAL ____________________

Credit Card *Tracker*

JAN ○ FEB ○ MAR ○ APR ○ MAY ○ JUN ○ JUL ○ AUG ○ SEP ○ OCT ○ NOV ○ DEC ○

DATE	CREDIT CARD	CREDIT LIMIT	% RATE	AMOUNT DUE	AMOUNT PAID	BALANCE

Monthly Financial *Reflection*

JAN ○ FEB ○ MAR ○ APR ○ MAY ○ JUN ○ JUL ○ AUG ○ SEP ○ OCT ○ NOV ○ DEC ○

TOTAL INCOME	TOTAL EXPENSES	DIFFERENCE	BALANCE

Biggest Wins this Month

What am I grateful for?

What do I need to improve for next month?

What did I learn by tracking my finances this month?

Wish *List*

JAN ○ FEB ○ MAR ○ APR ○ MAY ○ JUN ○ JUL ○ AUG ○ SEP ○ OCT ○ NOV ○ DEC ○

WISH LIST	HOPE TO PAY	WHERE TO BUY	BOUGHT	SPENT	SAVED	NOTES
			☐			
			☐			
			☐			
			☐			
			☐			
			☐			
			☐			
			☐			
			☐			
			☐			
			☐			
			☐			
			☐			
			☐			
			☐			
			☐			
			☐			
			☐			
			☐			
			☐			
			☐			
			☐			
			☐			
			☐			

Emergency Fund *Tracker*

JAN ○ FEB ○ MAR ○ APR ○ MAY ○ JUN ○ JUL ○ AUG ○ SEP ○ OCT ○ NOV ○ DEC ○

Amount Needed ____________ Target Date ____________

Monthly Savings Target ____________ Account ____________

Progress Tracker

10%	20%	30%	40%	50%	60%	70%	80%	90%	100%

DATE	DEPOSIT	WITHDRAW	NOTES	BALANCE

Notes

Credit Networking and *Mentorship*

JAN ○ FEB ○ MAR ○ APR ○ MAY ○ JUN ○ JUL ○ AUG ○ SEP ○ OCT ○ NOV ○ DEC ○

Networking Goals

What specific goals do you have for networking this month?

1 ______________________________

2 ______________________________

3 ______________________________

Mentorship Goals

What do you want to achieve with the help of a mentor this month?

1 ______________________________

2 ______________________________

3 ______________________________

Identify Networking Opportunities

Events & Workshops

List credit-related events, workshops, or webinars to attend this month:

1 ______________________________

2 ______________________________

3 ______________________________

Online Communities

Identify online groups or forums where you can engage with others focused on credit improvement:

1 ____

2 ____

3 ____

Track Your Progress

Networking Activities

Record your networking activities for the month (e.g., events attended, new connections made):

1 ____

2 ____

3 ____

Mentorship Activities:

Record your interactions with mentors (e.g., meetings, advice received):

1 ____

2 ____

3 ____

Notes

____

____

____

Charity and *Giving*

JAN ○ FEB ○ MAR ○ APR ○ MAY ○ JUN ○ JUL ○ AUG ○ SEP ○ OCT ○ NOV ○ DEC ○

DONATION	ORGANIZATION	DATE GIVEN	VALUE	TAX DEDUCTIBLE

Self-care and Financial *Health*

JAN ○ FEB ○ MAR ○ APR ○ MAY ○ JUN ○ JUL ○ AUG ○ SEP ○ OCT ○ NOV ○ DEC ○

Self-Care Reflection

- **Physical Well-being**

  What physical health activities will you focus on this month?

  o ____________________

  o ____________________

- **Emotional & Mental Wellness**

  What mental health activities will you focus on this month?

  o ____________________

  o ____________________

- **Time for Self-Care**

  How will you make time for yourself?

  o ____________________

  o ____________________

Financial Health Reflection

- **Current Financial Practices**

  What financial habits do you want to maintain or improve this month?

  o ____________________

  o ____________________

- **Financial Goals**

  List your financial goals for this month

  - ____________________
  - ____________________

- **Financial Self-Care**

  How will you manage financial stress?

  - ____________________
  - ____________________

Accountability & Progress

- **Support System**

  Who will help you stay accountable this month?

  - ____________________
  - ____________________

- **Tracking Progress**

  How will you monitor your progress? (e.g., weekly check-ins, journaling)

  - ____________________
  - ____________________

- **End-of-Month Review Date**

  Set a date to review your goals and make any necessary adjustments

  - ____________________

December

SMART Financial Goals *Worksheet*

JAN ○ FEB ○ MAR ○ APR ○ MAY ○ JUN ○ JUL ○ AUG ○ SEP ○ OCT ○ NOV ○ DEC ○

Description of Goals	**SPECIFIC** Cost	**MEASURABLE** Monthly Amount	**ATTAINABLE** Method/Steps	**REALISTIC** Goal Length	**TIMEBOUND** Your Timeline

Notes

Credit Score *Tracker*

JAN ○ FEB ○ MAR ○ APR ○ MAY ○ JUN ○ JUL ○ AUG ○ SEP ○ OCT ○ NOV ○ DEC ○

Current Score ______ **Goal Score** ______

900

850

800

750

700

650

600

550

500

450

400

350

300

WEEK 1 WEEK 2 WEEK 3 WEEK 4

Monthly Budget *Planner*

JAN ○ FEB ○ MAR ○ APR ○ MAY ○ JUN ○ JUL ○ AUG ○ SEP ○ OCT ○ NOV ○ DEC ○

INCOME	AMOUNT
TOTAL	

BILLS	AMOUNT
TOTAL	

SAVINGS	AMOUNT
TOTAL	

EXPENSES	AMOUNT
TOTAL	

DEBT	AMOUNT
TOTAL	

SUMMARY	AMOUNT
INCOME	
BILLS	
SAVINGS	
EXPENSES	
DEBTS	
TOTAL	

Bills Payment *Calendar*

JAN ○ FEB ○ MAR ○ APR ○ MAY ○ JUN ○ JUL ○ AUG ○ SEP ○ OCT ○ NOV ○ DEC ○

SUN	MON	TUE	WED	THU	FRI	SAT

Debt Repayment *Plan*

JAN ○ FEB ○ MAR ○ APR ○ MAY ○ JUN ○ JUL ○ AUG ○ SEP ○ OCT ○ NOV ○ DEC ○

Creditor

Debt Type

Starting Balance

Credit Limit

Repayment Frequency

Interest Rate

Goal Pay Off Date

Min Repayment

DATE	REPAYMENT	BALANCE	NOTES

Expense *Tracker*

JAN ○ FEB ○ MAR ○ APR ○ MAY ○ JUN ○ JUL ○ AUG ○ SEP ○ OCT ○ NOV ○ DEC ○

DATE	DESCRIPTION	AMOUNT	NOTES

TOTAL ______________________

Credit Card *Tracker*

JAN	FEB	MAR	APR	MAY	JUN	JUL	AUG	SEP	OCT	NOV	DEC
○	○	○	○	○	○	○	○	○	○	○	○

DATE	CREDIT CARD	CREDIT LIMIT	% RATE	AMOUNT DUE	AMOUNT PAID	BALANCE

Monthly Financial *Reflection*

JAN ○ FEB ○ MAR ○ APR ○ MAY ○ JUN ○ JUL ○ AUG ○ SEP ○ OCT ○ NOV ○ DEC ○

TOTAL INCOME	TOTAL EXPENSES	DIFFERENCE	BALANCE

Biggest Wins this Month

What am I grateful for?

What do I need to improve for next month?

What did I learn by tracking my finances this month?

Wish *List*

JAN ○ FEB ○ MAR ○ APR ○ MAY ○ JUN ○ JUL ○ AUG ○ SEP ○ OCT ○ NOV ○ DEC ○

WISH LIST	HOPE TO PAY	WHERE TO BUY	BOUGHT	SPENT	SAVED	NOTES
			☐			
			☐			
			☐			
			☐			
			☐			
			☐			
			☐			
			☐			
			☐			
			☐			
			☐			
			☐			
			☐			
			☐			
			☐			
			☐			
			☐			
			☐			
			☐			
			☐			
			☐			
			☐			
			☐			
			☐			

Emergency Fund *Tracker*

JAN ○ FEB ○ MAR ○ APR ○ MAY ○ JUN ○ JUL ○ AUG ○ SEP ○ OCT ○ NOV ○ DEC ○

Amount Needed ______ Target Date ______

Monthly Savings Target ______ Account ______

Progress Tracker

10%	20%	30%	40%	50%	60%	70%	80%	90%	100%

DATE	DEPOSIT	WITHDRAW	NOTES	BALANCE

Notes

Credit Networking and *Mentorship*

JAN ○ FEB ○ MAR ○ APR ○ MAY ○ JUN ○ JUL ○ AUG ○ SEP ○ OCT ○ NOV ○ DEC ○

Networking Goals

What specific goals do you have for networking this month?

1 ______________________________

2 ______________________________

3 ______________________________

Mentorship Goals

What do you want to achieve with the help of a mentor this month?

1 ______________________________

2 ______________________________

3 ______________________________

Identify Networking Opportunities

Events & Workshops

List credit-related events, workshops, or webinars to attend this month:

1 ______________________________

2 ______________________________

3 ______________________________

Online Communities

Identify online groups or forums where you can engage with others focused on credit improvement:

1 ____

2 ____

3 ____

Track Your Progress

Networking Activities

Record your networking activities for the month (e.g., events attended, new connections made):

1 ____

2 ____

3 ____

Mentorship Activities:

Record your interactions with mentors (e.g., meetings, advice received):

1 ____

2 ____

3 ____

Notes

Charity and *Giving*

JAN ○ FEB ○ MAR ○ APR ○ MAY ○ JUN ○ JUL ○ AUG ○ SEP ○ OCT ○ NOV ○ DEC ○

DONATION	ORGANIZATION	DATE GIVEN	VALUE	TAX DEDUCTIBLE

Self-care and Financial *Health*

JAN ○ FEB ○ MAR ○ APR ○ MAY ○ JUN ○ JUL ○ AUG ○ SEP ○ OCT ○ NOV ○ DEC ○

Self-Care Reflection

- **Physical Well-being**

  What physical health activities will you focus on this month?

  ○ ______________________________

  ○ ______________________________

- **Emotional & Mental Wellness**

  What mental health activities will you focus on this month?

  ○ ______________________________

  ○ ______________________________

- **Time for Self-Care**

  How will you make time for yourself?

  ○ ______________________________

  ○ ______________________________

Financial Health Reflection

- **Current Financial Practices**

  What financial habits do you want to maintain or improve this month?

  ○ ______________________________

  ○ ______________________________

- **Financial Goals**

  List your financial goals for this month

  - ______________________________
  - ______________________________

- **Financial Self-Care**

  How will you manage financial stress?

  - ______________________________
  - ______________________________

Accountability & Progress

- **Support System**

  Who will help you stay accountable this month?

  - ______________________________
  - ______________________________

- **Tracking Progress**

  How will you monitor your progress? (e.g., weekly check-ins, journaling)

  - ______________________________
  - ______________________________

- **End-of-Month Review Date**

  Set a date to review your goals and make any necessary adjustments

  - ______________________________

Glossary of *Terms*

Annual Percentage Rate (APR): The yearly interest rate charged on borrowed money, expressed as a percentage. It includes fees or additional costs associated with the transaction.

Authorized User: Someone who is allowed to use another person's credit card but is not responsible for paying the bill. Being an authorized user can help build credit history.

Balance Transfer: The process of moving debt from one credit card to another, usually to take advantage of a lower interest rate.

Bankruptcy: A legal process for individuals or businesses that are unable to repay their outstanding debts. It can have a severe impact on your credit score.

Charge-Off: When a creditor writes off a debt as unlikely to be collected after a certain period of missed payments. It negatively impacts your credit score.

Collateral: An asset that a borrower offers to a lender to secure a loan. If the borrower defaults, the lender can seize the collateral.

Cosigner: A person who signs a loan agreement with the borrower and agrees to repay the debt if the borrower defaults. Having a cosigner can help secure a loan if the borrower's credit is not strong enough.

Credit: The ability to borrow money or access goods or services with the understanding that you will pay later.

Credit Bureau: An organization that collects and maintains individual credit information and sells it to lenders, creditors, and consumers in the form of a credit report. Examples include Equifax, Experian, and TransUnion.

Credit Counseling: Professional advice and assistance to help individuals manage their debt and improve their financial situation.

Credit History: A record of a person's borrowing and repayment activities over time. It is used by lenders to determine creditworthiness.

Credit Limit: The maximum amount of credit a lender will extend to a borrower on a credit card or line of credit.

Credit Monitoring: A service that tracks your credit report for any changes or suspicious activity, often providing alerts for potential fraud.

Credit Report: A detailed report of an individual's credit history prepared by a credit bureau. It includes information on credit accounts, payment history, and public records.

Credit Score: A numerical representation of a person's creditworthiness based on their credit history. Common scoring models include FICO and VantageScore.

Credit Utilization Ratio: The amount of credit you're using compared to your total available credit, expressed as a percentage. Keeping this ratio low can positively impact your credit score.

Default: Failure to repay a loan according to the agreed terms. This can severely damage your credit score and make it difficult to obtain credit in the future.

Debt Consolidation: Combining multiple debts into a single loan with a lower interest rate, making it easier to manage payments.

Debt Settlement: Negotiating with creditors to reduce the amount of debt owed. It can have a negative impact on your credit score.

Finance Charge: The total cost of borrowing money, including interest and any fees.

Foreclosure: The legal process by which a lender takes possession of a property when the borrower fails to make mortgage payments.

Grace Period: The time between the end of a billing cycle and the date your payment is due. During this period, no interest is charged if the balance is paid in full.

Hard Inquiry: A credit check performed by lenders when you apply for a loan or credit card. It can slightly lower your credit score.

Identity Theft: The fraudulent use of someone's personal information, such as Social Security number or credit card details, to obtain credit or other benefits.

Installment Credit: A type of credit that is repaid in fixed payments over a set period of time, such as a car loan or mortgage.